Writing the Critical Essay

DRUNK DRIVING

An OPPOSING VIEWPOINTS® Guide

Lauri S. Friedman, *Book Editor*

Christine Nasso, *Publisher, Series Editor*
Elizabeth Des Chenes, *Managing Editor*

OPPOSING
VIEWPOINTS®
SERIES

GREENHAVEN PRESS
An imprint of Thomson Gale, a part of The Thomson Corporation

THOMSON
GALE

Detroit • New York • San Francisco • New Haven, Conn. • Waterville, Maine • London

For more information, contact
Greenhaven Press
27500 Drake Rd.
Farmington Hills, MI 48331-3535
Or you can visit our Internet site at http://www.gale.com

LIBRARY OF CONGRESS CATALOGING-IN-PUBLICATION DATA

Drunk driving / Lauri S. Friedman, book editor.
   p. cm. — (Writing the critical essay)
  Includes bibliographical references and index.
  ISBN-13: 978-0-7377-3581-9 (hardcover)
  1. Drunk driving—United States. 2. Drunk driving—United States—Prevention.
  3. Essay—Authorship. I. Friedman, Lauri S.
  HE5620.D72D782 2008
  363.12'5140973—dc22

                                      2007031378

ISBN-10: 0-7377-3581-3 (hardcover)
Printed in the United States of America

CONTENTS

Section Three: Supporting Research Material

Examining the state of writing and how it is taught in the United States was the official purpose of the National Commission on Writing in America's Schools and Colleges. The commission, made up of teachers, school administrators, business leaders, and college and university presidents, released its first report in 2003. "Despite the best efforts of many educators," commissioners argued, "writing has not received the full attention it deserves." Among the findings of the commission was that most fourth-grade students spent less than three hours a week writing, that three-quarters of high school seniors never receive a writing assignment in their history or social studies classes, and that more than 50 percent of first-year students in college have problems writing error-free papers. The commission called for a "cultural sea change" that would increase the emphasis on writing for both elementary and secondary schools. These conclusions have made some educators realize that writing must be emphasized in the curriculum. As colleges are demanding an ever-higher level of writing proficiency from incoming students, schools must respond by making students more competent writers. In response to these concerns, the SAT, an influential standardized test used for college admissions, required an essay for the first time in 2005.

Books in the Writing the Critical Essay: An Opposing Viewpoints Guide series use the patented Opposing Viewpoints format to help students learn to organize ideas and arguments and to write essays using common critical writing techniques. Each book in the series focuses on a particular type of essay writing—including expository, persuasive, descriptive, and narrative—that students learn while being taught both the five-paragraph essay as well as longer pieces of writing that have an opinionated focus. These guides include everything necessary to help students research, outline, draft, edit, and ultimately write successful essays across the curriculum, including essays for the SAT.

Using Opposing Viewpoints

This series is inspired by and builds upon Greenhaven Press's acclaimed Opposing Viewpoints series. As in the parent series, each book in the Writing the Critical Essay series focuses on a timely and controversial social issue that provides lots of opportunities for creating thought-provoking essays. The first section of each volume begins with a brief introductory essay that provides context for the opposing viewpoints that follow. These articles are chosen for their accessibility and clearly stated views. The thesis of each article is made explicit in the article's title and is accentuated by its pairing with an opposing or alternative view. These essays are both models of persuasive writing techniques and valuable research material that students can mine to write their own informed essays. Guided reading and discussion questions help lead students to key ideas and writing techniques presented in the selections.

The second section of each book begins with a preface discussing the format of the essays and examining characteristics of the featured essay type. Model five-paragraph and longer essays then demonstrate that essay type. The essays are annotated so that key writing elements and techniques are pointed out to the student. Sequential, step-by-step exercises help students construct and refine thesis statements; organize material into outlines; analyze and try out writing techniques; write transitions, introductions, and conclusions; and incorporate quotations and other researched material. Ultimately, students construct their own compositions using the designated essay type.

The third section of each volume provides additional research material and writing prompts to help the student. Additional facts about the topic of the book serve as a convenient source of supporting material for essays. Other features help students go beyond the book for their research. Like other Greenhaven Press books, each book in the Writing the Critical Essay series includes bibliographic listings of relevant periodical articles, books, Web sites, and organizations to contact.

Writing the Critical Essay: An Opposing Viewpoints Guide will help students master essay techniques that can be used in any discipline.

Can Smart Technologies Prevent Drunk Driving?

Drunk driving has been a problem in the United States for decades; since cars became popular in the early 1900s, drunk driving has claimed the lives of hundreds of thousands, and injured millions more. As with many social problems, the twenty-first century offers groundbreaking, revolutionary technological solutions to old problems such as drunk driving. Such technologies, known as "smart technologies," have those who study drunk driving wondering if they have finally found a lasting solution to the problem.

A popular smart technology device increasingly believed able to prevent drunk drivers from getting behind the wheel of their car is the ignition interlock device (IID). The IID works by requiring a driver to breathe into a machine attached to their car before allowing the car's ignition to be started. Essentially, the device forces the driver to submit to a breathalyzer test right in their car. As of 2007, eighteen states had made installation of the devices mandatory for drunken driving crimes, and many others require the device to be installed on a case-by-case basis. New Mexico governor Bill Richardson has hailed the device, saying: "An interlock device is like a mechanical probation officer on duty and monitoring DWI [driving while intoxicated] offenders 24 hours per day and seven days per week. It's a wonderful device. It's going to dramatically curb DWI."[1]

Yet others worry that assigning smart technology human responsibilities is not a reliable or effective way to curb drunk driving. For one, not everyone ordered to install an IID in their car actually follows through on the order. Secondly, a drunk driver could simply have a sober person breathe into

---

[1] Quoted in Haya el Nasser, "States Turn on to Idea of Ignition Locks," *USA Today*, June 23, 2005.

the IID on their behalf, as has happened in several cases. Finally, a wide range of environmental factors could tamper with the IID's effectiveness. Lawrence Taylor, lead attorney in the largest law firm in the nation handling driving under the influence cases, writes: "IIDs are inaccurate, easily circumvented, dangerous—and ineffective. . . . IIDs are primitive devices that are mounted along with the ashtray in the car's dashboard—and thus subject to contaminants, cigarette smoke, vibrations from the road, etc. In any event, an intoxicated person could easily have someone else breathe into the device, or simply borrow or rent another car. And because IIDs generally require periodic retesting of the driver while the car is underway, the risk from driver distraction alone poses a very real danger."[2]

Another technology thought to reduce the problem of drunk driving is the alcohol-monitoring ankle bracelet. This device is attached to a person's ankle and monitors their blood chemistry levels for traces of alcohol. One such device called SCRAM (Secure Continuous Remote Alcohol Monitor) takes hourly readings of a person's sweat and evaluates the samples for alcohol consumption. Data from the bracelets is sent each morning to officials. Supporters of such bracelets believe it is a foolproof way to ensure that those who have been repeatedly busted for drunk driving do not drink and drive. "There's no fooling the SCRAM device," said Associate Circuit Judge Terry Cundiff. "You can't avoid it. It's around your ankle. It's your sweat. We know if it's been cut."[3]

Yet others are unconvinced that SCRAM and other bracelets are effective tools against drunk drivers. One reason is that SCRAM bracelets may not be 100 percent accurate. They are designed to identify ethanol from a person's sweat, but may identify ethanol from other substances that have alcohol in them, such as perfume, cologne, hair spray, alcohol-

[2] Lawrence Taylor, "Technology Alone Won't Tackle Drunk Driving: Ignition Interlock Devices Promoted by MADD Will Do Little to Stop people from Driving While Intoxicated," *Business Week Online*, December 4, 2006.
[3] Kim Bell, "Ankle Bracelet Can Catch DWI Offenders Who Cheat," *St. Louis Post-Dispatch*, January 23, 2006.

based cold medicines, and paint from spray-paint canisters. SCRAM manufacturers say they have developed methods to avoid misidentification; for example, those who are made to wear the ankle-monitoring bracelet must sign a document agreeing to refrain from using certain cold medicines and colognes. But others are wary of SCRAM's ability to tell the difference between alcohol measurements from drinking and from environmental factors. Attorney Patrick T. Barone says: "There are no published research studies confirming that the SCRAM device can distinguish between [alcohol from] drinking and non-drinking."[4]

However controversial, there are many who believe these technologies are the key to reducing—even someday eliminating—drunk driving injuries and fatalities. The American public is clearly interested: A poll reported in *Business Week Online* in 2006 revealed that 85 percent of the public supports mandatory installation of IIDs in the vehicles of repeat

A representative of the National Highway Traffic Safety Administration (NHTSA) encourages technology advancement to decrease the number of drunk driving occurrences.

4 Patrick T. Barone, "Alcohol Monitoring Ankle Bracelets: Junk Science or Important Scientific Breakthrough?" *Champion*, May 2005.

National president of Mothers Against Drunk Driving, Millie Webb, lost her daughter to a drunk driver. She actively supports using new technologies such as the ignition interlock device (IID) to reduce drunk driving.

drunk driving offenders, and 65 percent support mandatory installation for first-time offenders. The poll also revealed that Americans in general support advances in smart technologies to prevent drunk driving by a four-to-one margin. Thus, the key to reducing drunk driving for some is to put technology to use where other methods have failed. Glynn Birch, an author whose son Courtney was killed by a drunk driver in 1988, writes: "With current ignition interlocks and future technology, we finally have the ability to separate potential killers—drunk drivers—from their weapon, an automobile. We must use it. Just like in a courtroom drama, the prosecution rests. The verdict: Interlocks and new technology will save lives."[5]

Yet others believe that smart technology is a superficial and temporary fix to a problem that has deeper roots. They argue that while technology can be used as an aid to prevent some drunk drivers from using their cars, it should not be relied upon to do what therapy, education, and treatment can: Eliminate the chronic and repetitive alcoholism that causes most drunk driving accidents. With this in mind, penalizing drunk drivers instead of treating them will never get to the heart of the problem. For this reason, attorney Lawrence Taylor and others believe that punishments for drunk driving should be rehabilitative instead of punitive. As Taylor puts it, "the choice is fairly simple: Do you want vengeance, or safety? Would you prefer to have a chronic drunk driver off the road for a few months —or in control of his disease?"[6]

Whether smart technologies can reduce the problem of drunk driving has yet to be conclusively determined, but it is certain that drunk driving—and new technologies to prevent it will continue to be debated by those who seek a solution to the problem. What causes drunk driving, what effects it has on society, and how to prevent it are enduring topics of study covered in *Writing the Critical Essay: An Opposing Viewpoints Guide: Drunk Driving.*

5 Glynn Birch, "Tapping Technology to Battle Drunk Driving: Ignition Interlock Devices Can Be a Powerful Tool in Keeping Repeat Offenders from Getting Behind the Wheel While Intoxicated," *Business Week Online,* December 12, 2006.
6 Taylor, "Technology Alone Won't Tackle Drunk Driving."

Section One:
Opposing
Viewpoints on
Drunk Driving

Drunk Driving Is a Serious Problem

Lucinda Dillon Kinkead

In the following viewpoint, author Lucinda Dillon Kinkead discusses how drunk driving is increasing among teenagers. Through the stories of Utah teenagers, she shows that peer pressure causes many teens to engage in underage drinking. When they get behind the wheel, says Kinkead, the results are disastrous. In fact, the number of teens arrested for drunk driving in Utah has doubled each year since 2001. Kinkead reports that lawmakers, social workers, and educators believe it is important to invest in counseling programs that will dissuade teens from binge drinking and driving in order to save their lives and the lives of others.

Lucinda Dillon Kinkead is a reporter for the *Deseret Morning News*, a newspaper based in Salt Lake City from which this viewpoint was taken.

Consider the Following Questions:

1. According to the author, illegal underage drinking accounts for what percentage of all alcohol consumed in the United States?
2. How many underage drunk drivers were arrested in Utah in 2003, according to the author? How many in 2002?
3. Why did Taylorsville, Utah, need to start a special program to handle juvenile driving-under-the-influence cases?

Tony can't believe now how much time he's wasted in his 13 years—time spent sitting in a basement with some of his so-called friends, skipping school and drinking vodka.

Lucinda Dillon Kinkead, "Wasted Youth: More Teens Yield to Lure of Alcohol," *Deseret Morning News*, March 28, 2004. Copyright © 2004 Deseret News Publishing Company. Reproduced by permission.

He hooked up with booze two years ago, when the older brother of a friend called him names because he didn't want to drink. "So I got drunk and I liked it," said Tony. He was 11 that first time. Today he's 13, locked up in one of the state's youth corrections programs for the crimes he committed while under the influence.

"I Did It with No Hesitation"

Thomas is a little older, 16. He was trying to walk on to Granger High School's football team one day last fall, but some friends asked him to come party with them instead. He never made the tryout. He was probably lost by then anyway, he says, on the road to big-time trouble. He was a bully—a husky, mean guy who learned when he was in the ninth grade how to throw his size and his attitude around.

"I'd just walk up to someone. 'You got a dollar?' I'd hit any kid because I knew I was never going to get in trouble. I knew they were never going to tell." He'd take the money, buy beer or sometimes marijuana, skip school and head over to a nearby abandoned house and get wasted.

But he got cocky. One day he downed a bottle of gin and juice at school. "I did it with no hesitation, but I got caught."

He's locked up on charges of assault, tampering with a witness's testimony, drinking at school and trespassing. . . .

The Power of Peer Pressure

It never crossed Tony's mind, when he first began drinking at age 11, whether the alcohol was damaging his brain. Thomas wasn't worried about going to detention or jail. . .

Instead, . . . they were concerned only with impressing their friends, feeling important and fitting in.

And this is the reality facing Utah educators and advocates in the fight against underage drinking: Peer pressure

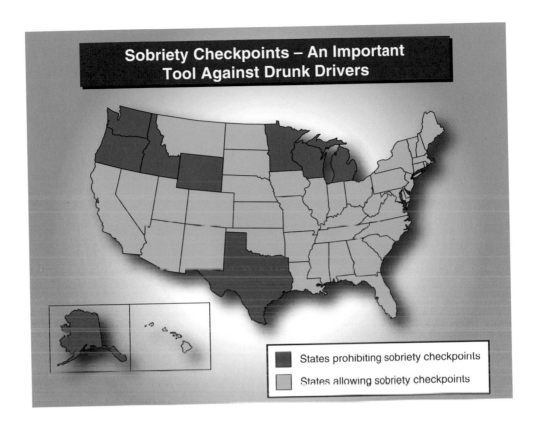

Sobriety Checkpoints – An Important Tool Against Drunk Drivers

States prohibiting sobriety checkpoints

States allowing sobriety checkpoints

is a powerful intoxicant, too, and more young people in the Beehive State are succumbing to the lure.

"This business of the notion that drinking is a rite of passage has just got to go," said Art Brown, president of the Utah chapter of Mothers Against Drunk Driving, who is leading a renewed effort to battle underage drinking in Utah with messages delivered to Utah schools, courtrooms and offender programs.

More Teens Arrested for Driving Under the Influence

It is true that Utah teens drink less than their peers around the country, but a number of factors have parents, educators and advocates worried.

The percentage of teens who use alcohol climbed from 17.9 percent to 21 percent between 2001 and 2003, according to the 2003 Utah Public Health Outcome Measures Report

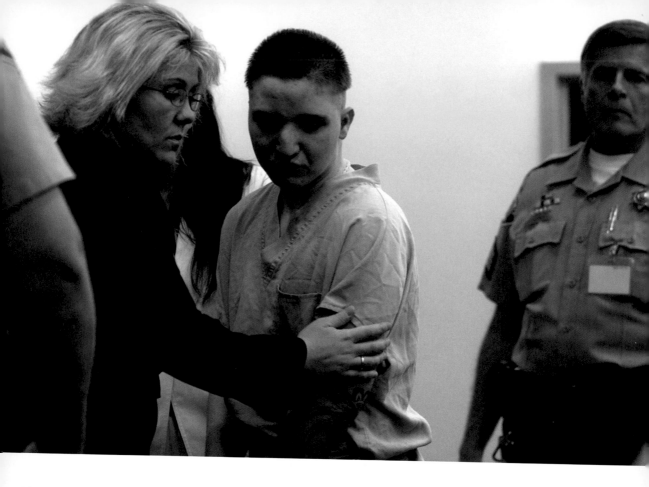

Teenager Tory Jacques was charged in 2003 with a second degree felony in Salt Lake City, Utah. He was driving under the influence of alcohol and killed a six-year old.

issued by the Utah Department of Health in December 2003.

Fourteen percent of Utah high school students—about 22,000 kids—have five or more drinks of alcohol in a row, according to a state survey that evaluated behavior during the past 30 days [March 2004].

This "binge drinking" behavior costs Utah $36 million a year, in public expenses and medical costs, according to Utah Population and Utah Office of Education figures.

Illegal underage drinking accounts for up to 20 percent of all alcohol consumed in the United States, according to a recent report from the American Medical Association.

Drunken driving among teenagers is increasing. In 2001, 362 people between 15 and 20 were arrested for driving under the influence [DUI] in Utah, according to the Utah Highway Safety Office. That number nearly doubled in 2002, when 668 people of the same age were arrested for DUI. In 2003, 1,256 youth were arrested for DUI.

Consumption and Crashes on the Rise

Alcohol-related crashes caused by teenage drivers are at an all-time high according to Utah's Crash Outcome Data Evaluation System Intermountain Injury Control Research Center at the University of Utah.

Although Utah's schools report fewer alcohol and substance abuse violations than last year, 1,357 students were arrested for drinking or drug offenses in 2002–2003, according to a report just released [in 2004] by the Utah State Office of Education. . . .

Judge Michael Kwan, who runs a special drug and alcohol program in Taylorsville's Justice Court, . . . believes underage consumption is on the rise—and it doesn't help that authorities sometimes do not recognize the potential harm and treat the offense with appropriate seriousness, he said.

"A 'slap on the wrist' really just encourages future abuse as it reinforces the attitude that the individual doesn't have a problem and that society doesn't think their abuse is a serious problem."

Special Programs to Help Teen Drunk Drivers

DUI offenders who are 16 and 17 years old are handled in a juvenile court, but minors charged with the consumption or possession of alcohol have risen so sharply that Taylorsville started a special program to handle the cases, [Judge Kwan] said. This program includes an assessment to determine the severity of abuse and education or counseling, random drug and alcohol testing and monthly court reports.

A recent school survey showed more than 45 percent of Utah students find alcohol is the easiest illegal substance to obtain, with 21.1 percent of 12th-graders reporting that they used alcohol in the past 30 days. The same survey, the Student Health and Risk Prevention Survey, published at the end of 2003, shows on average youth first try alcohol around age 12.

Trying to Save a Life

Kimberly Clift, who works at a convenience store on Foothill Boulevard, says teenagers are becoming more bold about trying to buy booze, including generating false identification on their home computers.

"I see kids trying to buy beer with fake IDs all too often," she said. "When they do try, I take the ID from them, write down the license plate number of their car and call the cops."

She's not sure prosecutors or law enforcement officers do much about it, but she believes she's doing a good thing.

"The reason why I take the ID from them is because I see it as saving a life," Clift said. "I am preventing them from drinking and driving and probably killing someone in an accident. . . ."

Tony and Thomas say it was no problem to obtain alcohol or drugs. They'd make beer runs or get alcohol from older friends or relatives.

"You can pretty much get anything you want, anytime you want," Thomas said. . . .

Preventing Underage Drunk Driving

Prevention does seem to be the key, and the [State Division of Substance Abuse] recently was awarded a federal grant for substance abuse prevention activities at Utah's colleges and universities. Underage drinking and drinking and driving are just two of the areas that will be addressed in the program, to be kicked off in September [2004]. . . .

Brown and others hope this renewed focus on underage drinking will lead to a more thorough examination of how law enforcement works to enforce underage drinking issues.

For example, . . . Tony and Thomas . . . are part of a program in the state's Division of Youth Corrections that

If you are on the
9:30 calendar &
want an attorney

evaluates kids to see what treatment or punishment is most appropriate for them.

The Observation and Assessment Center is a 45-day program where young people get a psychiatric evaluation, a medical check, an assessment of their educational abilities and 24-hour observation. Counselors talk about addictions, anger management and family issues. Offenders go to school. . . .

Teenager Carlos Rodolfo Preito pled guilty to killing three members of the Ceran family on December 24, 2006, while driving drunk.

"A Second Chance"

At the end of the 45 days, the program recommends the best course of action for a youth offender. Some will go to a lockdown secure facility like Decker Lake. Others who have made progress may go to proctor homes—much like foster homes—and then back home.

"It's like a second chance," says Thomas.

The counselors there tell it to them straight, Tony says. "They tell us, 'This is what you can do in life if you stop drinking and doing all this stuff. Look how good you can be. Look how famous you can be."

Tony wants to get back on that football team. Thomas says he's young, and pretty smart. "I could go to college."

Analyze the Essay:

1. In this viewpoint, the author discusses the role that peer pressure plays in underage drinking and driving. Is there peer pressure to drink and drive at your school? If so, how do you handle it? Are there programs at your school that have had success in making teens aware that drinking and driving is a fatal combination?

2. This viewpoint used narrative elements to make its point that drunk driving is a serious problem. Identify these narrative elements and explain whether or not you found them compelling.

Drunk Driving Is Not a Serious Problem

Ed Haas

In the following viewpoint, author Ed Haas argues that the problem of drunk driving has been exaggerated. He claims that the number of deaths supposedly caused by drunk drivers is inflated by misleading statistics and inaccurate data. When fatalities are called "alcohol-related," he explains, that does not mean that anyone was legally drunk, only that someone involved was believed to have consumed alcohol. In addition, Haas says, the vast majority of people who die in alcohol-related accidents are the drinkers themselves, and do not threaten the rest of society the way some claim.

Haas is the editor of the *Muckraker Report,* a news and opinion Web site that reports on a variety of issues.

Consider the Following Questions:

1. What does the author consider to be an accurate percentage of alcohol-related traffic fatalities?
2. According to the viewpoint, what is the legal blood alcohol concentration (BAC) limit in most states?
3. In what percentage of alcohol-related fatalities is the involvement of alcohol not verified by testing, according to the author?

The National Highway Traffic Safety Administration [NHTSA] defines a fatal traffic crash as being alcohol-related if either a driver or a non-occupant (e.g., pedestrian) has a blood alcohol concentration (BAC) of 0.01 grams per deciliter (g/dl) or greater in a police-reported traffic crash.

Ed Haas, "NHTSA Computation Methods: Misleading Statistics and How Such Have Influenced Our Current DUI Law and Encouraged the Institution of Suspicionless Seizures Described as Sobriety Checkpoints," Muckraker-Report.org, February 15,

To put 0.01 g/dl in perspective, ten times that amount is required to achieve a BAC of 0.10 g/dl, which is the legal limit of intoxication in most states.

"Alcohol-Related" Does Not Always Mean Drunk

Simply put, if a legally sober driver is involved in a traffic accident in which another legally sober person is killed, and the person killed happened to drink one beer 30 minutes prior to the accident, the NHTSA will classify that fatality as alcohol-related and consequently, that particular fatality will be deceptively employed to bolster statistics designed to fortify the perception that mindless, epidemic-type numbers of drunk drivers are blindly hurling down our highways,

A lab technician tests an Intoxilyzer 8000 machine, which can read a person's blood alcohol concentration (BAC) to determine if one is indeed intoxicated enough to be considered drunk.

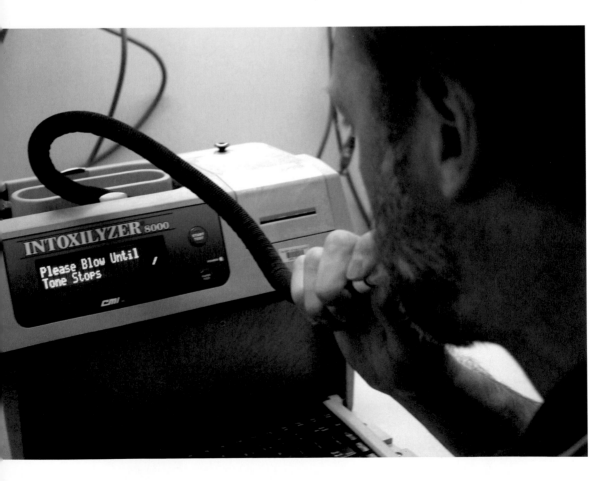

aimlessly killing innocent bystanders. These same statistics are then implemented into a continual effort to persuade the legislature to enact ever increasingly stringent DUI [driving under the influence] laws and more severe punishments.

To further illustrate, there were 16,653 alcohol-related traffic fatalities in 2000, according to the NHTSA. Of these 16,653 alcohol-related fatalities, 12,892 involved at least one driver or non-occupant with a BAC of 0.10 g/dl or greater. 7,326 were the intoxicated drivers themselves, and 1,594 were legally intoxicated pedestrians and pedal-cyclists. The remaining 3,972 fatalities were non-intoxicated drivers, passengers, and non-occupants. So how many actual victims of drunk driving were there in 2000?

Statistics Don't Measure Guilt

Excluding the 7,326 legally intoxicated drivers and 1,594 legally intoxicated pedestrians/pedal-cyclists, there remain 3,972 fatalities; but even these deaths cannot be classified as

While the idea of giving her keys to a designated driver was a good one, Gloria still wasn't thinking straight.

DUI: Profile of Repeat Offenders

Mothers Against Drunk Driving has identified the following traits that are possessed by most repeat drunk drivers:

- ■ Repeat offenders were found to **drink in multiple locations**.

- ■ **Beer** was the drink of choice for offenders.

- ■ 40% were **more likely to drink at a party** than at home.

- ■ Most convicted DUI offenders **believed they were not impaired** when arrested.

- ■ **17% of bar patrons** had been cited for DUI.

- ■ Repeat offenders were more likely to have a **prior criminal history**. (More moving and nonmoving violations and more single-vehicle and alcohol related accidents.)

- ■ **Typical repeat offender**: Male, under 40, white, low income, unmarried, no college, blue collar, alcohol problems, blood alcohol content slightly higher than first offender.

Taken from: Mothers Against Drunk Driving (Utah Chapter)

victims because the NHTSA does not indicate which driver was at fault. For example, if a sober driver runs a red light and crashes into a driver who has a BAC of 0.10 or greater, and the sober driver dies, the NHTSA will proclaim that this fatality is alcohol-related, even though alcohol had nothing to do with the crash, and tragically, the intoxicated driver will potentially face vehicular manslaughter charges. Law enforcement will wrongfully conclude that the drunk driver is at fault, and more likely than not, will not execute a thorough traffic scene investigation. Essentially, if alcohol is involved, it is disorderly to blame. Meanwhile, organizations such as MADD are spoon-fed this fatality, and they in turn inappropriately use it to mislead our lawmakers.

Former U.S. Senator Mike DeWine used beer cans as a prop while arguing in favor of a bill to lower the legal blood-alcohol limit from .10 to .08 in Ohio.

Unfortunately, the deception does not end there. According to the NHTSA, on an average, in more than 50 percent of the reported alcohol-related fatalities, alcohol involvement, as determined by actual alcohol testing, is not known. Alcohol test results may not be known for any of several reasons: the test was given but the results were not obtained by the Fatality Analysis Reporting System (FARS); the test was refused; FARS was unable to determine if test were given; or, the test was not given. As a result, the NHTSA imputes alcohol involvement in over 50 percent of the reported alcohol-related traffic fatalities. Imputation, as applied by NHTSA, uses characteristics of the persons involved in the crash to predict alcohol involvement when it is not known. Those characteristics include police-reported drinking, age, sex, restraint-use, type of crash, time of day, and driver of striking or struck vehicle. Sadly, these predicted, unsubstantiated, fatalities are masqueraded as confirmed victims of drunk driving, and have had an unjust role in the shaping of DUI laws across America, along with serving as justification to erode the Fourth Amendment protecting against unreasonable search and seizure without probable cause, by the establishment of sobriety checkpoints. . . .

There Are Few Innocent Victims

Remember, 50 percent of these fatalities are predicted due to lack of actual alcohol testing. Additionally, approximately 15 percent of the alcohol-related traffic fatalities involve no driver or pedestrian who is legally intoxicated; that one or more of the participates had a measurable amount of alcohol in their blood, but were below the legal limit within their given states. That being said, realistically the percentage of substantiated alcohol-related traffic fatalities is approximated 12.5 percent, with approximately 65 percent of these fatalities being the driver themselves.

Certainly statistics vary from state to state, but rest assured that the same distortion is occurring wherever you may reside. Also, it is important to remember that approximately 65 percent of all alcohol-related traffic fatalities are in fact the driver

> **Drunk Driving Laws Are Unfair**
>
> Our [drunk driving] laws should be grounded in sound science and the presumption of innocence, not in hysteria. They should target repeat offenders and severely impaired drunks, not social drinkers who straddle the legal threshold.
>
> Radley Balko, "Drunk Driving Laws Are Out of Control," Cato Institute, July 27, 2005.

themselves, so the actual percentage of innocent victims of drunk driving is minimal, compared to the leading cause of traffic fatalities on our nations highways: Speed! . . .

Over 1.5 million U.S. citizens are arrested each year for DUI. For over 20 years now, these citizens have fallen victim to the propaganda surrounding their crime, while their respective states inflict unjust punishments upon them.

Analyze the Essay:

1. The author cites a different set of statistics to argue that the problem of drunk driving has been exaggerated. What is your interpretation of his use of these statistics? Do they help prove his point, or serve to muddle his argument? Do you think they indicate that drunk driving is a serious problem, or not?

2. Haas argues that the number of "innocent" victims in drunk driving accidents—that is, those involved in alcohol-related accidents who are not drunk themselves—is very small. In your opinion, how concerned should society be with protecting those who drink from the consequences of their own actions?

Harsher Laws for Teens Can Prevent Drunk Driving

Wendy Cole Henderson

In the following viewpoint, author Wendy Cole Henderson explores whether instituting harsher laws for teenage drivers could prevent drunk driving among youth. Henderson reports that teenage drivers are four times more likely than adults to get into a fatal car crash. With numbers like these, she argues, stronger limits on adolescent driving may prevent thousands of teenage deaths each year. Imposing curfews, age limits, and other restrictions on teenage drivers could help them avoid driving after drinking at parties, she argues. Though many parents think their child will not drink and drive, Henderson presents evidence from one family to show that teenage drunk driving can devastate without any notice.

Wendy Cole Henderson is a freelance author. Her articles have appeared in *Time* magazine, from which this viewpoint was taken.

Consider the Following Questions:

1. Describe the circumstances of Sean Larimer's car crash, as reported by the author.
2. According to the author, what did researchers at the National Institute of Mental Health discover about teenage brains?
3. What results have graduated driver licensing (GDL) laws had on teen drivers, according to the author?

Since kindergarten, they had been known as "the crew." Still a close-knit group in high school, the five Henderson, Nev., boys were all delighted when Sean Larimer turned 16 and in 2003 became the first to get his driver's license. Sean's mom, Susan Larimer, a hospital nurse who was in the midst of a divorce, was happy about it too. "I thought I needed him to drive," she recalls. So Susan gave her son permission to drive around with the crew one evening just 63 days after he passed his road test.

Every Parent's Worst Nightmare

As was customary during his outings with friends, Susan and Sean checked in with each other by cell phone several times. But while awaiting his return, Susan dozed off. Just after 1 A.M., the phone startled her awake with the news every parent of a teen dreads. Her son had smashed her '98 Pontiac Grand Am and was in the hospital's trauma unit. Three of the boys in the car had been killed, the fourth injured. Sean, who had been drinking heavily at a party that night (reportedly as much as eight beers in an hour), served two years in juvenile lockup for driving under the influence of alcohol and reckless driving. He cannot get his license back until he turns 21. Susan, shaken by the tragedy and determined to spare other young drivers and their parents similar agony, has lobbied state lawmakers to make the licensing process for teen drivers lengthier and more safety conscious. "I'm not making excuses for his choice to drink," she says. "But if we had tougher laws"—like prohibiting newly licensed teens from transporting other minors—"Sean would not have been out driving with his friends that night." In October 2005, Nevada put in place a graduated licensing law, which phases in driving privileges as teens gain experience and maturity.

Massachusetts State Police Lt. Paul Maloney holds an Ignition Interlock Device (IID), which prevents an automobile from being started without a breath sample.

Teens May Not Be Ready to Drive

Getting a driver's license remains a signal milestone for teens in their impatient journey toward adulthood—and for their parents, eager to liberate themselves from constant chauffeuring duties. But car crashes are the main cause of death for U.S. teenagers, killing about 6,000 drivers between the ages of 16 and 19 each year. That's more fatalities for this age group than those caused by guns and drug overdoses combined. And the younger and less experienced the driver, the worse the danger. Drivers ages 16 to 19 have a fatality rate four times as high as that of drivers 25 to 29.

Experts say that parents who assume that simply reminding their kids to buckle up and watch the speed limit miss the central problem: the adolescent brain may be unable to handle the responsibilities of driving. Researchers with the National Institute of Mental Health have shown that the parts of the brain that weigh risks, make judgments and control impulsive behavior are still developing through the teen years and don't mature until about age 25.

Stricter Licensing Laws

Those findings—and aggressive lobbying by auto-safety advocates—have helped push 45 states to adopt some form of graduated driver licensing, or GDL, which lengthens the waiting period before teens can obtain a full "go anywhere, anytime" driver's license. Slowing down the process has slowed down the accident rate. Per-capita crashes have fallen 23% among 16-year-old drivers in California since its strict GDL law was enacted in 1998, the Insurance Institute for Highway Safety (IIHS) reported in August [2006]. The state's late-night crashes were down 27%, and crashes with teen passengers were down 38%. Similar drops have occurred in other states. Despite those impressive results, however, legislators have balked at imposing additional measures that could make teen drivers even safer.

Combating Teenage Drunk Driving

Studies of zero tolerance laws indicate they reduce crashes among drivers younger than 21. A study of 12 states that passed zero tolerance laws reported a 20 percent reduction in the proportion of fatal crashes that were single-vehicle nighttime events (crashes likely to involve alcohol impairment) among drivers ages 15–20.

Insurance Institute for Highway Safety, "Q & A: Teenagers—Underage Drinking," 2006.

Studies suggest that nighttime driving is particularly dangerous for teens, and curfews are urged. "Most accidents involving teens occur before midnight," says Susan Ferguson, senior vice president of research for the IIHS. "So the smartest laws go into effect earlier." But last year [2005] nine states introduced measures to rein in teens' nighttime driving privileges, and only one—Nevada—passed such a law. "A lot of adults think, I used to drive at night with my friends, so what's the harm?" says Judith Lee Stone, president of the nonpartisan Advocates for Highway and Auto Safety in Washington. "It's hard to change people's thinking unless there's a crash involving someone they know. Then people get it immediately." This year [2006] six states—Arizona, Florida, Iowa, Michigan, Ohio and Kentucky—have considered new or additional nighttime restrictions, but only Kentucky's bill passed, propelled, in part, by the death of the 17-year-old granddaughter of state representative Tom Burch of Louisville, who was the sponsor.

Keeping Teens Out of Cars to Reduce Drunk Driving

Nevada is one of the last states to join the decade-long movement to restrict teen drivers, but its law is now among the most comprehensive in the nation. It requires teen drivers to be off the road by 10 P.M., earlier than the midnight or 1 A.M. curfews in other states (six states still have no nighttime limits at all). Nevada also set a six-month waiting period between permit and licensing, mandates at least 50 hours of parent-supervised driving experience that must be tracked in a written log, and forbids newly licensed drivers to transport other youths for three months. "The more teens in the car, the greater the risk," says Ferguson. Goofy, adolescent yammering in the backseat isn't the only distraction posing a threat. Ferguson says the mere presence of peers can induce kids to take risks they otherwise wouldn't, often because they're trying to impress their passengers.

The changes are already producing positive results. In Las Vegas, collisions involving teen drivers were down 18%, to 1,155, for the first eight months of [2006] compared with the same period in 2005. In the Larimers' hometown of Henderson (pop. 250,000), there have been two fatalities, but only one teen has been ticketed for violating the driving curfew, and not one has been nabbed for illegally carting around friends. Police admit that they are more likely to call parents than write up a violation, believing that a more informal approach is as much a deterrent as sending the family through the court system.

"It Can Happen to Anyone"

Some parents are ambivalent about the law and are not convinced that the restrictions should apply to their children. Becky Jeffries of Las Vegas, whose daughter Kristilyn, 17, had three fender benders in the first year she was licensed, doubts that enforcing the 10 P.M. curfew will keep her

An ignition interlock device (IID) is used by breathing directly into it. It then generates a reading of whether someone is drunk or sober.

Common Characteristics of Drunk Drivers

One study found that compared to all drivers, drunk drivers tend to be more aggressive, hostile and thrill seeking. They are more likely to have a criminal record, to use drugs and to have poor driving records, and to even have severe mental health problems. These and the following attributes are shared by repeat offenders:

Mean Age	35
Education	High school or less
Occupation	Non-white collar
Income	Low
Other Offenses	Traffic and criminal
Gender	Male (over 90 percent)
Race	White
Marital Status	Unmarried
BAC	> 0.18 percent at arrest; higher in fatal crashes
Prior DWIs	2–3
Alcohol Problems	Alcohol dependency common

Taken from: National Hardcore Drunk Driver Project

daughter any safer. "She's not going to get any better by being held back. She might as well be in control of her own destiny," Becky says.

Donna Botti and her daughter Angela, 16, share those sentiments. On a recent Saturday evening as Angela was getting ready for a friend's sweet-16 party at a downtown Vegas club, she belatedly noticed the phrase "Parent Drop-off and Pickup Preferred" on her invitation. "How stupid is that? I have my own car," she scoffed. Although the festivities were supposed to end at 10 P.M., Angela had no intention of racing home in her shiny '05 Hyundai Tucson to make curfew. In fact, she and her parents said they were unaware that nighttime restrictions for teens existed until being interviewed for this story. Donna's sunny expression momentarily turned pained when she was asked whether she would allow Angela, who was chauffeuring two pals that evening, to ignore the law: "I don't want to feel like an uncaring mother, but truthfully, I'm not worried about her."

That kind of statement makes Susan Larimer cringe. "People would like to believe Sean's crash was an isolated incident," she says. "But the second your kid drives away under his or her own power, you have no idea what can happen. If this nightmare can happen to our family, it can happen to anyone."

Analyze the Essay:

1. Most teens are able to get their driver's license by the age of 16 or 17. But in this viewpoint, the author presents evidence that 16 and 17 year olds may not be ready to handle the responsibility, and are at greater risk of making fatal mistakes such as drinking and driving. What do you think? Are teens capable of driving without restrictions? Or might licensing restrictions help them adjust to the responsibility of driving? Explain your answer and suggest ways you might reduce drunk driving through licensing laws.

2. This viewpoint used narrative elements to make the point that harsher driving limits on teenagers could reduce drunk driving. Identify these narrative elements and explain how you think they enhanced the article.

My Husband Was Killed by a Drunk Driver

Faith L. Konsdorf

In the following viewpoint, widow Faith L. Konsdorf tells the story of her husband Bill, who died following a drunken driving accident. The car crash was so devastating that Bill had to be airlifted to the hospital, where he drifted into a coma. Konsdorf remembers sitting by her husband's side, praying he would wake up from his coma. Eventually, however, it became clear that Bill would not wake up, and his wife describes how she realized she had to let him go. Bill died eight days after his alcohol-related crash. Konsdorf shares her story in the hopes that others will be inspired to refrain from drinking and driving and to support antidrunk driving groups such as Mothers Against Drunk Driving (MADD), which published Konsdorf's story.

Consider the Following Questions:
1. What decision was the author asked to make regarding her comatose husband?
2. According to the author, what affect did her presence have on her husband while he was in a coma?
3. On what day did the author's husband die?

I had always tried to write my book of life in chapters, but when I met Bill it didn't really belong to just me anymore. Suddenly, it became "Our Book of Life" and it was writing and rewriting itself every minute.

Faith L. Konsdorf, "Book of Life: A Grieving Widow Gains Strength From the Power of Love," *MADDvocate*, spring 2006, pp. 22–23. Reproduced by permission.

State Look Back Periods

A "look back" period is how long states look back at drunk driving offenses.

24–36 Months	5 Years	6–9 Years	10 Years	12 Years	15 Years	Lifetime
*Navajo Nation	AL, AS, AZ, DE, GA, Guam, *HI, ID, IN, *KS, KY, MD, MS, *MO, MT, *ND, Northern Marian Islands, Puerto Rico, RI, *WI, WY	*AK, *MI, *NE, NV, NC, *ND, *OH, PA, WA	*AK, CN, *HI, IL, LA, ME, *MA, *MI, MN, *MO, NH, NJ, NM, NY, OK, OR, SC, SD, TN, TX, UT, VA, Virgin Islands, WV	IA, *NE	Washington, DC	American Samoa, CO, FL, *KS, *MA, *OH, VT, *WI

*States with more than one look back period:
AK - 10 years on 2nd and subsequent offenses, 6 years for felony DUI on 3rd and subsequent offenses
HI - 5 years on a 2nd offense, 10 years for felony DUI on 4th and subsequent offenses
KS - 5 years on 2nd and subsequent offenses, lifetime for felony DUI on 3rd and subsequent offenses
MA - 10 years on 2nd offense, lifetime on 3rd and subsequent offenses
MI - 7 years on a 2nd offense, 10 years on 3rd and subsequent offenses
MO - 5 years on a 2nd offense, 10 years on 3rd and subsequent offenses
NE - 8 years on 2nd and subsequent offenses, 12 years for sentencing purposes
ND - 5 years on 2nd and 3rd offenses, 7 years on 4th offenses
OH - 6 years on 2nd and subsequent offenses, lifetime for 3rd degree felony DUI on 5th and subsequent offenses
WI - 5 years on a 2nd offense, lifetime on 3rd and subsequent offenses

Taken from: National Hardcore Drunk Driver Project

"A Bond That Even We Couldn't Explain"

Our life was great. We had little things specific only to us. Eating Chinese take-out by candlelight. Sliding down our driveway in the snow on pizza pans at 3 A.M. Watching every sunrise and sunset we could together. Our Valentine's Day pranks were the best. Bill and I were everything to one another. We had a bond that even we couldn't explain. We were husband and wife, best friends and lovers, and couldn't stand to be away from each other. We were so close that even the things that happened to us were in sync.

A Vermont state trooper inspects the damage of a wrecked car four teenagers died in when returning from a night of drinking in Quebec, Canada.

So on March 22, 2004, when he hadn't called and he wasn't answering his cell phone, I knew something was wrong. I could feel it.

Stolen by Drunk Driving

Finally Bill's phone was answered, but not by my beloved husband. Instead, the police officer who answered told me that Bill had been involved in a horrific alcohol-related crash. He had been airlifted to the hospital, where he was in a coma and on life support.

Several days after the crash, I was asked to make the hardest decision of my life: whether or not to take Bill off of life support. I couldn't make this decision, especially without Bill. We made our decisions together.

In tears, I ran to the chapel, prayed and remembered something Bill had said when our best friend was dying. Bill said, "Never let a machine keep me alive. Let God take me when he wants." I cried selfish tears because I wanted to keep him with me, but I knew I had to do what Bill wanted.

I went back up and gave the approval to take him off life support. I held his hand the whole time. I was told if he couldn't breathe on his own, he would pass in 15 minutes. I watched as his chest rose and fell. He was breathing on his own.

Holding on for Love

Several days later, while he was still in a coma, all the monitors went off. I knew this was it. I jumped in bed with him, held him tight and prayed.

The doctor came in and said, "I have no idea what kind of bond the two of you have, but I've heard about 'the miracle couple' and it's certainly true. Everything at the nurses' station went off indicating that your husband's time was up. But something greater than a miracle happened. His oxygen saturation, vital signs and everything were almost gone, and you touched him and they got better. The two of you have something special, and the best medicine for your husband is you. So I've written an order to the effect that when you are in the hospital, which is always from what I hear, you need to be as close to him as you can be, lie with him, hold him."

He knew I was there and I cried happy tears.

Every night, I climbed in bed with him, snuggled up to him with my head on his chest just as if we were at home. I loved hearing his heartbeat.

> ## A Pain That Will Never Fully Heal
>
> The emotional aftermath of losing a loved one to impaired driving is filled with feelings and experiences. . . . Ultimately, what people are left with is sorrow. Sorrow encompasses the knowledge that you will always feel sadness over the tragic loss of your loved one; however, it also represents a step away from being overwhelmed by grief.
>
> Mothers Against Drunk Driving (MADD) Canada, "Making Sense of the Senseless: The Emotional Trauma of Losing a Loved One to Impaired Driving," March 9, 2005.

Learning to Let Go

Then, one night, something inside me made me stop in my tracks. I walked around to his side of the bed. I gently kissed his lips, hugged him tightly, held his head in my arms and whispered to him, "Bill, you know how much I love you and I love you more than anyone has ever loved anyone on this earth. You have no idea how much I want you to stay here with me. Holding on to you is the easiest thing I can do, but letting go, that's the hardest. But I realize that you aren't 100 percent mine. We are one; that is so true. I want you to stay with me more than I've ever wanted anything, but if you need to go, I understand and I will hold you in my heart and love you forever." I kissed him on the forehead and stepped back to go around to my side of the bed.

Suddenly, Bill's eyes opened. I started screaming for joy. But he was not back; he was gone. Bill was pronounced

To show the consequences of drunk driving, students from Burlington High School in Iowa simulate a pre-prom drunk driving accident.

dead after 2 A.M. on March 30, 2004. I crawled in bed with him, snuggled up to him and put my head on his chest just like every night. The only thing missing was his heartbeat.

After the funeral was over, it seemed everyone turned the page to the next chapter of their life: a life without Bill Konsdorf. I couldn't do that. Bill wasn't a page or a chapter. He was my Book of Life.

My "Book of Life"

My grief was overwhelming. Without Bill, I didn't think I would make it. But then I remembered something I said while delivering his eulogy. "Bill was full of life. If we are breathing, we have life and there is nothing more Bill would want to see than for those he loved and those he didn't even know to be happy and living their lives to the fullest."

Doing that was the greatest gift I could ever give him and that he could give me.

In life and in death, our love keeps me going. The miraculous bond we shared is what gives me purpose in life. It's not time, it's the love we share that heals. Bill has helped me through as only Bill could. He was my Book of Life. He wrote it with me and he still is helping me write it today.

Analyze the Essay:

1. This viewpoint differs from the other viewpoints in this section in that it is a first-person narrative, or someone's account of an event in their own words. In what way do first-person narratives differ from other types of essays? What are their strengths? What are their weaknesses?

2. Examine the dialogue contained in this essay. In your opinion, does it sound believable? Why or why not? Identify what you think works or does not work about it.

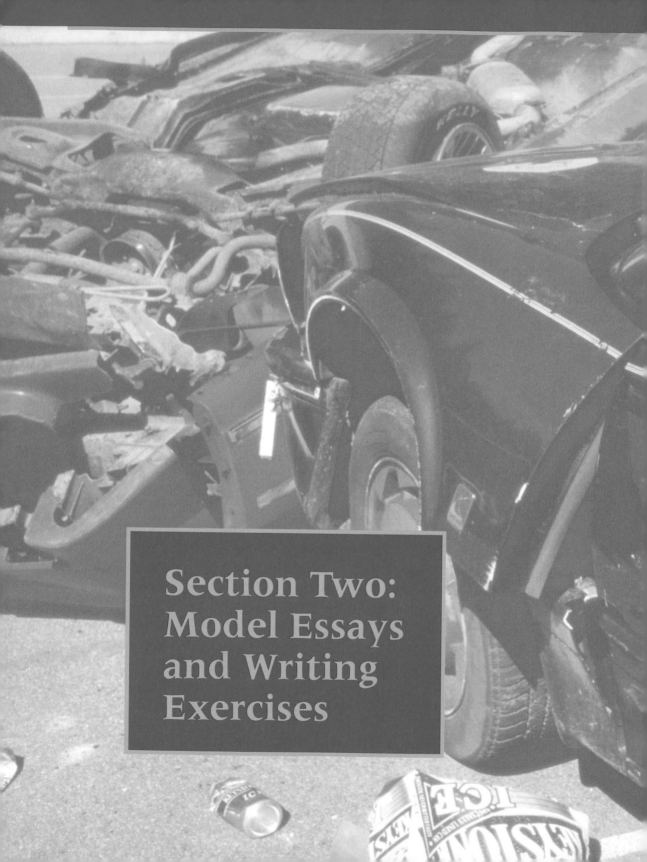

Section Two:
Model Essays
and Writing
Exercises

The Five-Paragraph Essay

An *essay* is a short piece of writing that discusses or analyzes one topic. The five-paragraph essay is a form commonly used in school assignments and tests. Every five-paragraph essay begins with an *introduction,* ends with a *conclusion,* and features three *supporting paragraphs* in the middle.

The Thesis Statement. The introduction includes the essay's thesis statement. The thesis statement presents the argument or point the author is trying to make about the topic. The essays in this book all have different thesis statements because they are making different arguments about drunk driving.

The thesis statement should clearly tell the reader what the essay will be about. A focused thesis statement helps determine what will be in the essay; the subsequent paragraphs develop and support the thesis statement.

The Introduction. In addition to presenting the thesis statement, a well-written introductory paragraph captures the attention of the reader and explains why the topic being explored is important. It may provide the reader with background information on the subject matter or feature an anecdote that illustrates a point relevant to the topic. It could also present startling information that clarifies the point of the essay or put forth a contradictory position that the essay will refute. Further techniques for writing an introduction are found later in this section.

The Supporting Paragraphs. The introduction is followed by three (or more) supporting paragraphs. These are the main body of the essay. Each paragraph presents and develops a *subtopic* that supports the essay's thesis statement. Each *subtopic* is spearheaded by a *topic sentence* and supported by its own facts, details, and examples. The writer can use various kinds of supporting material and details to back up the topic of each supporting paragraph. These may include statistics, quotations from people with special knowledge or expertise, historic facts, and anecdotes. A rule of writing is that specific and concrete examples are more convincing than vague, general, or unsupported assertions.

The Conclusion. The conclusion is the paragraph that closes the essay. Its function is to summarize or reiterate the main idea of the essay. It may recall an idea from the introduction or briefly examine the larger implications of the thesis. Because the conclusion is also the last chance a writer has to make an impression on the reader, it is important that it not simply repeat what has been presented elsewhere in the essay but close it in a clear, final, and memorable way.

Although the order of the essay's component paragraphs is important, they do not have to be written in the order presented here. Some writers like to decide on a thesis and write the introduction paragraph first. Other writers like to focus first on the body of the essay, and write the introduction and conclusion later.

Rules to Remember

When writing a narrative essay, there are a few common rules to remember. Writing a narrative essay is one of the few times it is appropriate to write in the first person. When attempting to tell a compelling story that has happened to you, it is acceptable to use "I." In addition, an author writing a narrative essay may also write more emotionally or descriptively than is appropriate for other kinds of essays. Normally, when writing persuasive or cause-and-effect essays, authors strive for an objective, professional tone. But because narrative writing features stories, it is acceptable to open your writing to a unique and personal writing style.

Also, when writing essays about controversial issues such as drunk driving, it is important to remember that disputes over the material are common, precisely because there are many different perspectives. Remember to state your arguments in careful and measured terms. Evaluate your topic fairly—avoid overstating negative qualities of one perspective or understating positive qualities of another. Use examples, facts, and details to support any assertions you make.

The Narrative Essay

Narrative writing is writing that tells a story or describes an event. Stories are something most people have been familiar with since childhood. When you describe what you did on your summer vacation, you are telling a story. Newspaper reporters write stories of daily events. Novelists write fictional stories about imagined events.

Stories are often found in essays meant to persuade. The previous section of this book provided you with examples of essays about drunk driving. Most are persuasive essays that attempt to convince the reader to support specific arguments about issues regarding drunk driving. In addition to making arguments, the authors of these essays also tell stories in which drunk driving plays a part. They used narrative writing to do this.

Components of Narrative Writing

All stories contain basic components of character, setting, and plot. These components answer four basic questions— who, when, where, and what—that readers need to make sense of the story being told.

Characters answer the question of whom the story is about. In a personal narrative using the first-person perspective ("I could never forgive the drunk driver who killed my brother."), the characters are the writer herself and the people she encounters. But writers can also tell the story of other people or characters ("Officer Thomas pulled over a drunk driver just before he drove the wrong way onto a highway entrance ramp.") without being part of the story themselves.

The setting answers the questions of when and where the story takes place. The more details given about characters and setting, the more the reader learns about them and the author's views toward them. Faith L. Konsdorf's description of her husband's hospital experience in Viewpoint 4 provides a good example of vividly describing the setting in which the story takes place.

The plot answers the question of what happens to the characters. It often involves conflict or obstacles that a story's character confronts and must somehow resolve. An example: Tracy Smith has to choose between driving home drunk or calling her parents for a ride. If she drives home, she may be able to hide the fact she was drinking; if she calls her parents, she may get home safely but risk being punished. How Tracy chooses to handle the situation will affect the outcome of the story.

Some people distinguish narrative essays from stories in that essays have a point—a general observation, argument, or insight that the author wants to share with the reader. In other words, narrative essays also answer "why" questions: Why did these particular events happen to the character? Why is this story worth retelling? The story's point is the essay's thesis.

Using Narrative Writing in Persuasive Essays

Narrative writing can be used in persuasive essays in several different ways. Stories can be used in the introductory paragraph to grab the reader's attention and to introduce the thesis. Stories can comprise all or part of the middle paragraphs that are used to support the thesis. They may even be used in concluding paragraphs as a way to restate and reinforce the essay's general point. Narrative essays may focus on one particular story, or may draw upon multiple stories.

A narrative story can also be used as one of several arguments or supporting points. Or, a narrative can take up an entire essay. Some stories are so powerful that by the time the reader reaches the end of the narrative, the author's main point is clear.

In the following section, you will read some model essays on drunk driving that use narrative writing. You will also complete exercises that will help you write your own narrative essays.

Living with the Guilt

Editor's Notes As you read in Preface B, narrative writing has several uses. Writers may incorporate the narrative technique into another type of essay, such as a persuasive essay or a compare-and-contrast essay. Instead of focusing their whole essay on a single story, they may use several different stories together. They may also choose to use narrative only in portions of their essay.

The following essay uses pieces of narration to discuss the experience of people who have driven drunk and seriously hurt or killed others. As you read, pay attention to the essay's components and how they are organized. Also note that all sources are cited using Modern Language Association (MLA) style. For more information on how to cite your sources see Appendix C.* In addition, consider the following:

1. How does the introduction engage the reader's attention?
2. How is narration used in the essay?
3. What purpose do the essay's quotes serve?
4. Would the essay be as effective if it contained only general arguments, and the stories of Reggie Stephey, Sean Larimer, and Scott A.S. Willeke were not included?

Refers to thesis and topic sentences

Refers to supporting details

Paragraph 1

Drunk drivers victimize themselves in addition to the people they injure and kill. In addition to strict penalties for drunk driving, such as jail sentences, hefty fines, and a criminal record, driving drunk can lead to mistakes that will haunt a person for the rest of their life. Indeed, the crushing guilt

* Editor's Note: In applying MLA style guidelines in this book, the following simplifications have been made: Parenthetical text citations are confined to direct quotations only; electronic source documentation in the works cited list omits date of access, page ranges, and some detailed facts of publication.

from harming or killing another person is a punishment that some describe as even worse than death. Three drunk drivers talk about how their tragic mistake will forever haunt them; yet there is nothing they can do to erase the pain they caused to so many people and themselves.

This is the essay's thesis statement; it tells the reader what the essay will be about.

Paragraph 2

Reggie Stephey is one person who has to live with the guilt of having destroyed the lives of others. When he was eighteen years old, Reggie drove drunk after a party and caused a horrific accident. He smashed his car into a vehicle carrying five people, causing a terrible wreck and a ghastly fire. One person was killed and three were injured. One of the injured—a girl named Jacqui Saburido—was so horrifically deformed, that she could no longer function normally. Reggie was sentenced to seven years in prison and was fined ten thousand dollars for the death he caused. At his trial, Reggie explained how he would always live with the guilt of his terrible mistake and described the damage he had caused as "a pain that will never go away" (qtd. in Hafetz, 27). Although he could never repair the lives he had destroyed, Reggie decided to dedicate his life to educating teenagers about drunk driving in the hopes they would be deterred from making the same irrevocable mistake he had.

Note the specific details and examples that are used to describe Reggie's story. Always use specific details rather than vague or general ones.

Paragraph 3

While some drunk drivers and their victims are strangers who never meet, some drunk drivers and their victims are friends or family. One such person who will have to live with the guilt of having harmed his loved ones is Sean Larimer, who got behind the wheel of a car very drunk one night in order to drive his four best friends home after a party. The group had been inseparable since kindergarten. But on that fateful night, Sean, who had had as many as eight beers in one hour, crashed the car and killed three of his friends and seriously injured the fourth. Sean was sentenced to two years in juvenile prison and lost his license for five years. However, none of these punishments could touch the

This is the topic sentence of paragraph three.

Transitional phrases help the author flow from one idea to another.

unsoothable remorse Sean felt for his crime. "People would like to believe Sean's crash was an isolated incident," says Sean's mother, Susan. "But the second your kid drives away under his or her own power, you have no idea what can happen. If this nightmare can happen to our family, it can happen to anyone" (qtd. in Henderson, 72).

This quote was taken from Viewpoint 3. Learn how to integrate powerful and useful quotes into your writing.

Paragraph 4

Another person who knows the horror of killing a loved one is Scott A.S. Willeke, who killed his wife by driving drunk. He took his wife out for a night of dancing and drinking, and thought he was sober enough to get them home in one piece. However, while navigating a curve he had driven hundreds of times before, Willeke lost control of the vehicle, slamming it into a concrete pole. His wife was thrown from the car and hit the pole, dying instantly. Willeke will never forgive himself for this tragedy, for which he was convicted of manslaughter. He writes from his jail cell, "Driving requires your best judgment and reflexes. Unfortunately, alcohol took mine away that night; and that took my wife away forever."

Specific, vivid details help your reader envision the scenario.

Paragraph 5

Some argue that it is inappropriate to feel sympathy for a drunk driver. After all, this person stole the lives of innocent others by being selfishly reckless. Yet drunk drivers are not like other criminals such as murderers or rapists, who intend to cause harm to their victims. Drunk drivers are usually people who do not set out intending to hurt anyone else. Victims of drunk drivers sometimes understand this. Jacqui Saburido, for example, acknowledged that Reggie did not intend to harm her or her friends. "I wish there was something between guilt and innocence," she said at his trial. "I don't hate you, but you need to understand that you committed a grave mistake" (qtd. in Hafetz, 26). Like most drunk drivers, Reggie will likely spend the rest of his life unable to forgive himself for the hurt and pain he caused to himself and so many others—and wishing he could undo his fateful mistake.

Note how the conclusion draws the essay's ideas to a close without simply repeating what has already been covered.

Vivid, personal quotes help enliven narrative essays.

Works Cited

Hafetz, David. "Chasing Hope." *Austin-American Statesman* May 2002: 27.

Henderson, Wendy Cole. "Putting Limits on Teen Drivers." *Time 23* Oct. 2006: 72.

Willeke, Scott A.S. "I Threw It All Away! I Killed My Wife by Driving Drunk." *Combat Edge* Apr. 2002.

Exercise 1A: Create an Outline from an Existing Essay

It often helps to create an outline of the five-paragraph essay before you write it. The outline can help you organize the information, arguments, and evidence you have gathered during your research.

For this exercise, create an outline that could have been used to write essay one: "Living with the Guilt." This "reverse engineering" exercise is meant to help familiarize you with how outlines can help classify and arrange information.

To do this you will need to:

1. articulate the essay's thesis;
2. pinpoint important pieces of evidence;
3. flag quotes that support the essay's ideas; and
4. identify key points that support the argument.

Part of the outline has already been started to give you an idea of the assignment.

Outline

I. Paragraph 1

A. Write the essay's thesis:

II. Paragraph 2

Topic: Reggie Stephey must live with the guilt of having destroyed the lives of others.

Supporting Detail A.

Supporting Detail B. Quote from Reggie expressing his emotions.

III. Paragraph 3

Topic:

A. Sean was sentenced to two years in juvenile prison and lost his license for five years.

B.

IV. Paragraph 4

Topic:

A.

B.

V. Write the essay's conclusion:

Drunk Driving Lockdown: The Advantage of Using Ignition Interlock Devices

Editor's Notes The second essay, also written in five paragraphs, is a slightly different type of narrative essay than the first essay. In the first essay, the author contrasted the stories of three different people to make a point about drunk driving. In the following essay, the author focuses on just one narrative story to argue that ignition interlock devices should be used to reduce drunk driving.

The notes in the sidebars provide questions that will help you analyze how this essay is organized and how it is written.

Paragraph 1

A small new weapon in the fight against drunk driving is proving to have big rewards. The weapon is a device called an ignition interlock. Ignition interlock devices are machines built into a car that prevent it from being started without a breath sample. If the driver's breath tests positive for a certain level of alcohol, the car's ignition will be locked, and the person will be prevented from driving drunk. Ignition interlock devices are steadily moving to the forefront of the war against drunk driving in the United States: and with good reason.

This is the essay's thesis statement. It tells the reader what the essay will be about. Each paragraph will relate in some way to this idea.

Paragraph 2

Consider the case of Eliza Smith, a New Mexico resident who was arrested in July 2005 for drunk driving. In previous years, Smith would have been arrested, forced to do community service, and sent on her way. But just prior to Smith's arrest, New Mexico became the first state to require ignition interlock devices installed on the cars of all first-time driving

The story of Eliza Smith is woven into the essay's argument. The narrative helps personalize the argument and bring it to life.

under the influence offenders. Under the new law, Smith was ordered by a judge to purchase the device (for one thousand dollars) and have it installed in her car.

Paragraph 3

You may be thinking, what is to stop Eliza Smith from simply having a sober person blow into the device to start the car if she is drunk? While not foolproof, ignition interlock devices have been designed to resist fraud or tampering. It is very difficult to fool them into accepting the breath of a sober person who will not be driving the car. For example, devices require not just an initial breath to start the car, but also random breath samples throughout the entire duration of the ride. This prevents a drunk person from having a sober person start the car for them and then taking off. Smith would be out of luck if her plan was to avoid the breathalyzer by having a sober person start her car for her.

> This is the topic sentence of paragraph three. Topic sentences do not always need to be the first sentence in a paragraph. They just have to contain the paragraph's main idea.

Paragraph 4

Unfortunately, only eighteen states currently have mandatory ignition interlock laws. Forty-three states and the District of Columbia have the option to make convicted drunken drivers use interlocks, but they are not always imposed. New Mexico was proud to become the first state to make installation of the device mandatory to prevent people like Eliza Smith from harming themselves or others. New Mexico governor Bill Richardson said of the program, "An interlock device is like a mechanical probation officer on duty and monitoring DWI [driving while intoxicated] offenders 24 hours per day and seven days per week. It's a wonderful device. It's going to dramatically curb DWI" (qtd. in el Nasser).

> Transitional statements like this one help keep the ideas in the essay moving forward.

> The author has quoted a state governor. Quoting high-profile people can lend legitimacy and authority to your essay.

Paragraph 5

There will always be Eliza Smiths out there who will put themselves and others at risk simply because they are too lazy to call a cab or get a ride from a sober friend. Ignition interlock devices help keep such people in check. All states should follow New Mexico's lead in making these devices a leading tool to curb drunk driving.

Works Cited

El Nasser, Haya. "States Turn on to Idea of Ignition Locks." *USA Today* 23 Jun 2005.

Exercise 2A: Create an Outline from an Existing Essay

As you did for the first essay in this section, create an outline that could have been used to write "Drunk Driving Lockdown: The Advantage of Using Ignition Interlock Devices." Be sure to identify the essay's thesis statement, its supporting ideas, its descriptive passages, and key pieces of evidence that are used.

Exercise 2B: Create an Outline for Your Own Essay

The second essay expresses a particular point of view about ignition interlock devices. It argues they should be used to prevent repeat drunk driving. For this exercise, your assignment is to find supporting ideas, choose specific and concrete details, create an outline, and ultimately write a five-paragraph essay making a different, or even opposing, argument about drunk driving. Your goal is to use narrative techniques to convince your reader.

Step I: Write a thesis statement.
The following thesis statement would be appropriate for an opposing essay on why ignition interlock devices do not always effectively reduce drunk driving:

> Ignition interlock devices are no silver bullet for preventing drunk driving—the devices can be tampered with; they do not prevent other types of substance-related crashes; and many offenders do not follow through with court orders to install them in their car.

Or, see the sample essay topics suggested in Appendix D for more ideas.

Step II: Brainstorm pieces of supporting evidence.

Using information from some of the viewpoints in the previous section and from the information found in Section III of this book, write down three arguments or pieces of evidence that support the thesis statement you selected. Then, for each of these three arguments, write down supportive facts, examples, and details that support it. These could be:

- statistical information
- personal memories or anecdotes
- quotes from experts, peers, or family members
- observations of people's actions or behaviors
- specific and concrete details

If you want to write an essay on the above thesis statement, a good place to look for supporting evidence is in the introduction to this book, "Can Smart Technologies Reduce Drunk Driving?" This essay discusses the effect smart technologies such as ignition interlock devices (IIDs) can have on drunk driving reduction. It contains the opinions of people who oppose using such technologies, such as Lawrence Taylor, the lead attorney in the largest law firm in the nation that handles driving under the influence cases, who said:

> IIDs are inaccurate, easily circumvented, dangerous—and ineffective. . . . IIDs are primitive devices that are mounted along with the ashtray in the car's dashboard—and thus subject to contaminants, cigarette smoke, vibrations from the road, etc. In any event, an intoxicated person could easily have someone else breathe into the device, or simply borrow or rent another car. And because IIDs generally require periodic retesting of the driver while the car is underway, the risk from driver distraction alone poses a very real danger.

Use this and other relevant pieces of information to support your argument.

Step III: Place the information you have so far in outline form.

Step IV: Write the arguments or supporting statements in paragraph form.

By now you have three arguments that support the essay's thesis statement, as well as supporting material. Use the outline to write out your three supporting arguments in paragraph form. Make sure each paragraph has a topic sentence that states the paragraph's thesis clearly and broadly. Then, add supporting sentences that express the facts, quotes, details, and examples that support the paragraph's argument. Each paragraph may also have a concluding or summary sentence.

Step V: Write an introduction and conclusion for your essay.

See Exercise 3B for information on writing introductions and conclusions. Then, write an introduction and a conclusion for the essay you have partially written via this exercise.

The Mistake That Lasted for Years

Editor's Notes The third narrative essay is similar to the essay you just read. It focuses on one story to make its point, instead of using small pieces of several different stories. However, instead of just being woven throughout the main argument, the story takes up most of the essay.

The following essay tells the story of Maria, who was severely punished after being caught drunk driving. The characters, setting, and plot are recounted in more detail than they would be in a simple anecdote in order to better engage the reader in the story. In this way the author relies on the power of the story itself to make the point that drunk driving can have serious consequences.

The notes in the margins provide questions that will help you analyze how this essay is organized and written.

Refers to thesis and topic sentences

Refers to supporting details

What is the essay's thesis statement? What language indicates this will be a narrative essay?

Paragraph 1

In addition to possibly harming yourself and others, you may suffer heavy consequences if you drive drunk. A drunk driver can lose his or her driver's license; spend time in jail; be forced to complete community service projects; and be subject to monitoring and surveillance programs that reduce their freedom and mobility. Sadly, many drunk drivers rarely begin the night intending to drive drunk. They make the ill-fated decision after drinking more than they planned and incorrectly assessing their driving ability. This is what happened to one woman named Maria Rigato, who learned the hard way that drunk driving is a mistake that takes minutes to make but takes years to recover from.

Paragraph 2

It was New Year's Eve, and Maria was living it up. The year 2006 was in the past; 2007 would be a year full of travel, excitement, and new opportunities. She was just sure of it. To celebrate Maria went to a friend's party. Although she considered taking a cab there, Maria wanted to save money; after all, she only planned on having a couple drinks and then going home shortly after midnight. But as the party went on, Maria lost count of how many drinks she had had. Then, someone brought out a brightly colored tray of Jello shots that tasted so sweet Maria could hardly believe there was a shot of vodka in each one! Before she knew it, it was 3 A.M. and she felt very tired and drunk. She had to get home. She considered calling a cab, but she didn't want to have to come get her car in the morning. "I'm fine to drive," she rationalized. "It's only a few miles anyway." Even though she had always looked down on those who got behind the wheel after drinking, Maria got in her car and pointed it in the direction of home.

> Paragraph 2 develops the main character's identity and establishes where the story takes place.

> Make a list of all transitional words and phrases used in the essay.

Paragraph 3

Peering blurrily through the windshield into the darkness, Maria began to feel sleepy. She was jarred awake suddenly by flashing lights ahead. What was this? she wondered. An accident? A towed car? Maria slowed the car to a halt and fumbled with her driver's side window. The cold night air hit her like a slap in the face. She looked hazily out the window and came face to face with a police officer. Maria had stumbled upon a sobriety checkpoint, a roadblock intended to screen drivers and catch those who may be driving under the influence. Indeed, sobriety checkpoints can be an effective tool for identifying and stopping drunk drivers before they hurt themselves or others. In the Florida county in which Maria lived, sobriety checkpoints were responsible for decreasing alcohol-related fatalities by 38.2 percent. Such results led the National Highway Traffic Safety Administration to conclude that "sobriety checkpoints are an

> This paragraph sets the plot in motion—the chronological actions and events that happen to the character.

> What specific details are included to help bring the essay to life?

effective law enforcement tool . . . to detect drivers impaired by alcohol and/or other drugs." (National Highway Traffic Safety Administration) On this New Year's Eve, the sobriety checkpoint had done exactly what it was supposed to. Maria was given a roadside sobriety test which included a breathalyzer test. Her blood alcohol content level (BAC) registered at 0.15 percent, well over the legal limit. Maria was immediately arrested for driving under the influence.

Paragraph 4

Paragraph 4 describes the events, actions, and consequences that stem from the pivotal event.

Although she hadn't hurt anyone, Maria was severely punished for putting herself and innocent people at risk. First, she lost her driver's license for up to one year, making it difficult for her to get to and from work, and essentially squashing her social life. Secondly, she was ordered to complete one hundred hours of community service at a hospital. Finally, she was ordered by a court of law to have an ignition interlock device installed in her car for at least five years. The device prevents Maria's car from starting without receiving a breath sample, which is analyzed for alcohol. It is intended to prevent her from making the mistake of thinking she is able to drive under the influence of alcohol again. "The ignition interlock system has literally prevented millions of starts and countless tragedies that could have ensued had an intoxicated driver been on the roadways" (Texas Safety Network, 1). In addition to being inconvenienced, Maria was humiliated every time she had to explain to a passenger what the device was.

This quote is taken from the Texas Safety Network, a reliable source. Practice supporting your essays with authoritative quotes from reliable sources.

Paragraph 5

How does the conclusion return to ideas discussed in the beginning of the essay?

On the whole, 2007 had not shaped up as Maria had expected. Instead of new travel, her mobility was tightly restricted; instead of new opportunities, she had new responsibilities of community service, and instead of excitement, she spent much time lamenting her decision to drive after drinking. Despite this, Maria felt thankful that she hadn't hurt herself or anyone else. She had learned a valuable lesson: When it comes to drinking and driving, it is never worth it.

Works Cited

National Highway Traffic Safety Administration. "Small Scale Sobriety Checkpoints." 2006. < www. nhtsa.dot.gov/people/injury/alcohol/StopImpaired/ YDDYLLaborDay/SmallScale.pdf > . Accessed March 15, 2007.

Texas Safety Network. "Ignition Interlock Device: Effective Tool Against Drunk Driving: Small Device Making Big Impact on DWIs." 4 Mar. 2005: 1.

Exercise 3A: Identifying and Organizing Components of the Narrative Essay

As you read in Preface B, narratives all contain certain elements, including characters, setting, and plot. This exercise will help you identify these elements and place them in an organized structure of paragraphs.

For this exercise you will isolate and identify the components of a narrative essay. The essay you just read, "The Mistake That Lasted for Years," is a good source to practice on. You may also, if you choose, use experiences from your own life or those of your friends.

Part A: Isolate and write down story elements.

Setting

The setting of a story is the time and place the story happens. Such information helps orient the reader. Does the story take place in the distant or recent past? Does it take place in a typical American community or an exotic locale?

Model Essay 2	Story taken from this volume	Other story
Maria is stopped at a sobriety checkpoint and arrested for drunk driving.		

Character

Who is the story about? If there is more than one character, how are they related? What stage of life are they in? What are their aspirations and hopes? What makes them distinctive and interesting to the reader?

Model Essay 2	Story taken from this volume	Other story
Maria Rigato Young woman in her 20s Likes to travel Hoped 2007 would be filled with new opportunities Needs car to get to work		

Pivotal Event

Most stories contain at least one single, discrete event on which the narrative hinges. It can be a turning point that changes lives or a specific time when a character confronts a challenge, comes to a flash of understanding, or resolves a conflict.

Model Essay 2	Story taken from this volume	Other story
Maria is stopped at a sobriety checkpoint and arrested for drunk driving.		

Events/Actions Leading up to the Pivotal Event

What are the events that happen to the characters? What are the actions the characters take? These elements are usually told in chronological order in a way that advances the action—that is, each event proceeds naturally and logically from the preceding one.

Model Essay 2	Story taken from this volume	Other story
Maria attends a party on New Year's Eve and drinks more than she planned. Because she does not want to pick up her car in the morning or pay for a cab, she tries to drive home.		

Events/Actions That Stem from Pivotal Event

What events/actions are the results of the pivotal event in the story? How were the lives of the characters of the stories changed?

Model Essay 2	Story taken from this volume	Other story
Maria is arrested, loses her license, is forced to do community service and have an ignition interlock device installed in her car.		

Point/Moral

What is the reason for telling the story? Stories generally have a lesson or purpose that is ultimately clear to the reader, whether the point is made explicitly or implied. Stories can serve as specific examples of a general social problem. They can be teaching tools describing behavior and actions that the reader should either avoid or emulate.

Model Essay 2	Story taken from this volume	Other story
Story is an example of the consequences of drunk driving.		

Part B: Write down narrative elements in paragraph form.

Since stories vary greatly, there are many ways to approach telling them. One possible way of organizing the story elements you have structured is as follows:

   Paragraph 1: Tell the reader the setting of the story and introduce the characters. Provide descriptive details of both.

   Paragraph 2: Begin the plot—what happens in the story. Tell the events in chronological order, with each event advancing the action.

Paragraph 3: Describe the pivotal event in detail and its immediate aftermath.

Paragraph 4: Tell the short-term and/or long-term ramifications of the pivotal event. This paragraph could also include the point or moral of the story.

Paragraph 5: Conclude the story in a memorable and interesting way.

Exercise 3B: Examining Introductions and Conclusions

Most essays feature introductory and concluding paragraphs that are used to frame the main ideas being presented. Along with presenting the essay's thesis statement, well-written introductions should grab the attention of the reader and make clear why the topic being explored is important. The conclusion reiterates the essay's thesis and is also the last chance for the writer to make an impression on the reader. Strong introductions and conclusions can greatly enhance an essay's effect on an audience.

The Introduction

There are several techniques that can be used to craft an introductory paragraph. An essay can start with:

- an anecdote: a brief story that illustrates a point relevant to the topic.
- startling information: facts or statistics that elucidate the point of the essay.
- setting up and knocking down a position: a position or claim believed by proponents of one side of a controversy, followed by statements that challenge that claim.
- historical perspective: an example of the way things used to be that leads into a discussion of how or why things work differently now.

- summary information: general introductory information about the topic that feeds into the essay's thesis statement.

Problem One
Reread the introductory paragraphs of the essays and of the viewpoints in Section I. Identify which of the techniques described above are used in the example essays. How do they grab the attention of the reader? Are their thesis statements clearly presented?

The Conclusion

The conclusion brings the essay to a close by summarizing or returning to its main ideas. Good conclusions, however, go beyond simply repeating these ideas. Strong conclusions explore a topic's broader implications and reiterate why it is important to consider. They may frame the essay by returning to an anecdote featured in the opening paragraph. Or, they may close with a quotation or refer back to an event in the essay. In opinionated essays, the conclusion can reiterate which side the essay is taking or ask the reader to reconsider a previously held position on the subject.

Problem Two
Reread the concluding paragraphs of the essays and of the viewpoints in Section I. Which were most effective in driving their arguments home to the reader? What sorts of techniques did they use to do this? Did they appeal emotionally to the reader or did they bookend an idea or event referenced elsewhere in the essay?

The Call That Saved My Life

Editor's Notes Essays drawn from memories or personal experiences are called personal narratives. The final essay is this type of narrative. It is not based on research or the retelling of someone else's experiences, such as the other narrative essays you have read in this book. Instead, this essay consists of an autobiographical story that recounts memories of an event that happened to the writer.

The essay differs from the first three essays in that it is written in the subjective or first-person ("I") point of view. It is also different in that it has more than five paragraphs. Many ideas require more than five paragraphs in order to be adequately developed. Moreover, the ability to write a sustained essay is a valuable skill. Learning how to develop a longer piece of writing gives you the tools you will need to advance academically. Indeed, many colleges, universities, and academic programs require candidates to submit a personal narrative as part of the application process.

As you read the following essay, take note of the sidebars in the margin. Pay attention to how the essay is organized and presented.

■ Refers to thesis and topic sentences

□ Refers to supporting details

Paragraph 1

There are some mistakes that you immediately forget, and there are others that will haunt you for the rest of your life. I learned this my senior year in high school, after attending a party with my best friend Amy—we did everything together. It was 1995, and we had just one semester before we went our separate ways to college. We were determined to have as much fun as possible before we graduated from high school.

Because this is a personal narrative, it does not have the type of thesis statement a more formal essay should have.

Paragraph 2

The party was one of the best I'd ever been to. My boy-friend's band played outside all night, and all of the coolest kids were there. Someone with a fake ID had managed to get three kegs, and I drank more beer than I ever had in my short life. Before I knew it, Amy and I were drunk and our curfew was rapidly approaching.

Paragraph 3

Does the dialogue sound natural to you? What details or features enhance it?

"Let's go dude, my dad will freak if I'm not home by 1 A.M.," Amy said. She pulled out her keys and stumbled toward her car.

"Are you seriously going to drive?" I said. "We've been drinking since like, 7 P.M. There is no way I could drive right now." As if to prove my point, I uncontrollably hiccupped.

"Don't be such a loser," she garbled. "We'll be fine. My house is like, four smiles from here. I mean, four miles. Ha!"

Paragraph 4

How is foreshadowing used in this paragraph? What purpose does it serve?

But something stopped me from getting in the car. Suddenly the end of the party felt like a bad episode of a television drama. I wasn't stupid; how many times had a character gotten busted for drunk driving—or worse?

Paragraph 5

What do you learn about the characters in these sentences? What kinds of people are they?

"What if we get arrested or something though! It's not worth it, dude. I'm just going to call my parents for a ride," I said.

"Don't be paranoid," said Amy, clearly exasperated with me. "You're only going to get yourself busted."

"I just think—"

"Whatever," she said. "Go call your mommy. Get in trouble. See if I care. Later loser!" With that, she drove off shakily into the night.

Paragraph 6

I was standing in the street all by myself. I took a deep breath, opened my cell phone, and called my parents. It rang just once—my mother, clearly awakened from a deep sleep, shouted frantically into the receiver, "Who is this? What's wrong?"

Paragraph 7

"Mom, don't worry, it's me." I explained that instead of going to the movies as I had told her, I was actually at a party and had been drinking. "Please don't be mad, Mom. I just—I just want you to come pick me up. Do you think you could pick me up?"

Are you interested in the characters and their motivations? Do they seem like real people to you? Personal narratives should strive for a realistic, natural tone.

Paragraph 8

She was there in twenty minutes. I was expecting a lecture, a freak out, an argument. But she was cooler than I ever could have imagined. "I'm disappointed you lied to me about what you were doing tonight," she said. "But I am glad you called me. Nothing you could do could ever make me so angry that I wouldn't want you to be safe."

Paragraph 9

The next morning I woke up with the worst headache I'd ever had. "So this is a hangover," I thought. I felt nauseous, exhausted, and weak. I spent all day in bed and missed the chance to see my boyfriend play in his soccer game. It would have been my only social event of the week; although they were pleased that I had called, my parents had grounded me from all social activities for two weeks because I had lied about my whereabouts. Plus, I was only allowed one phone call a day. When I felt better that afternoon, I used my call to phone Amy to see if her headache was as bad as mine.

A person's internal thoughts can help reveal character and advance the plot—what the character decides to do and why.

Paragraph 10

No one answered the phone at her house, so I tried her cell phone. But instead of Amy, I was surprised to get her mother. "Hey Mrs. Blair," I said. "Um, is Amy there? Did you guys switch phones or something?"

Paragraph 11

Her mother let out a deep wail. "Oh God," she said. "Honey, Amy's dead."

"What are you talking about?!" I started shaking so hard I thought I would never stop.

Paragraph 12

"She . . . she," Mrs. Blair paused to get her breath. "She apparently went to a party last night and tried to drive home drunk. But she never made it. She lost control of the car and drove into a tree. The police said her blood alcohol content was nearly twice the legal limit. I just can't believe this is happening. I can't believe my daughter is dead," she wailed.

Paragraph 13

"I can't either," I said. I felt numb. I hadn't been paranoid; calling my mother had saved my own life. And I would never see my friend again.

Paragraph 14

How does this paragraph serve to move the plot forward?

The next few months were difficult and sad. At her funeral, countless friends spoke about Amy's creativity, her sense of humor, her drive for life. I needed as many people as possible to know that Amy had been an incredible person whose life had ended much too soon. I worked on a committee to have a garden planted for her; to this day the flowers still bloom in the garden memorial at our old high school. Before graduating, I also began a Students Against Destructive Decisions (SADD) chapter at our school to help students learn from Amy's fatal mistake. It still exists and helps other students learn about being responsible about drinking and driving. At the end of the year when I left for college, I felt like I had done everything in my power to preserve Amy's memory, but nothing could ever really soothe the pain of losing my friend.

Paragraph 15

If I could change one thing in my life it would be to go back to that night and beg Amy to not drive home. She could have come home with me, endured some grounding, and lived. But I can't change the past. I can only live with the painful knowledge that the call that saved my life was not enough to save my friend's. I hope that others will learn from this story and internalize the important message: that drunk driving is never, ever, worth it.

Personal narratives are not expected to have a formal conclusion like other essays, but they must still tie the story's ideas to a close.

The previous essay used scene and dialogue to make a point. For this exercise, you will practice creative writing techniques to draft a one- or two-paragraph scene with dialogue. First, take another look at "The Call That Saved My Life" and examine how dialogue is used.

When writing dialogue, it is important to:

- Use natural-sounding language.
- Include a few details showing character gestures and expressions as they speak.
- Avoid overuse of speaker tags with modifiers, such as "he said stupidly," "she muttered softly," "I shouted angrily," and so on.
- Indent and create a new paragraph when speakers change.
- Place quotation marks at the beginning of and at the end of a character's speech. Do not enclose each sentence of a speech in quotation marks.

Scene Writing Practice

Interview a classmate, friend, or family member. Focus on a specific question about drunk driving, such as:

- Have you ever known anyone who has driven drunk? If so, why did they do it?
- Have you ever known anyone who has been in an accident caused by a drunk driver?
- What programs do you think might help reduce drunk driving?
- If you were offered a ride by a person who had been drinking, what would you do?

Take notes while you interview your subject. Write down what he or she says as well as any details that are provided. Ask probing questions that reveal how the subject felt, what they said, and how they acted. Use your notes to create a brief one- or two-paragraph scene with dialogue.

But I Can't Write That

One aspect of personal narrative writing is that you are revealing to the reader something about yourself. Many people enjoy this part of writing, but others have trouble with sharing their personal stories—especially if they reveal something embarrassing or something that could be used to get them in trouble. In these cases, what are your options?

- Talk with your teacher about your concerns. Will this narrative be shared in class? Can the teacher pledge confidentiality?
- Change the story from being about yourself to a story about a friend. This will involve writing in the third person rather than the first person.
- Change a few identifying details and names to disguise characters and settings.
- Pick a different topic or thesis that you do not mind sharing.

Write Your Own Five-Paragraph Narrative Essay

Using the information from this book, write your own five-paragraph narrative essay that deals with drunk driving. You can use the resources in this book for information about issues relating to drunk driving and how to structure a narrative essay. The following steps are suggestions on how to get started.

Step One: Choose your topic.

The first step is to decide what topic to write your narrative essay about. Is there an issue about drunk driving that particularly fascinates you? Is there an issue you strongly support or feel strongly against? Is there a issue you feel personally connected to? Ask yourself such questions before selecting your essay topic. Refer to the sample essay topics in Appendix D if you need help selecting a topic.

Step Two: Write down questions and answers about the topic.

Before you begin writing, you will need to think carefully about what ideas your essay will contain. This is a process known as *brainstorming*. Brainstorming involves asking yourself questions and coming up with ideas to discuss in your essay. Possible questions that will help you with the brainstorming process include:

- Why is this topic important?
- Why should people be interested in this topic?
- How can I make this essay interesting to the reader?
- What question am I going to address in this paragraph or essay?
- What facts, ideas, or quotes can I use to support the answer to my question?

Questions especially for narrative essays include:

- Have I chosen a compelling story to examine?
- Does the story support my thesis statement?
- What qualities do my characters have? Are they interesting?
- Does my narrative essay have a clear beginning, middle, and end?
- Does my essay evoke a particular emotion or response from the reader?

Step Three: Gather facts, ideas, and anecdotes related to your topic.

This book contains several places to find information, including the viewpoints and the appendixes. In addition, you may want to research the books, articles, and Web sites listed in Section III, or do additional research in your local library. You can also conduct interviews if you know someone who has a compelling story that would fit well in your essay.

Step Four: Develop a workable thesis statement.

Use what you have written down in steps two and three to help you articulate the main point or argument you want to make in your essay. It should be expressed in a clear sentence and make an arguable or supportable point.

Example:

Our school needs to create a Students Against Destructive Decisions (SADD) chapter to educate newly licensed teenagers about the dangers of drunk driving.

This could be the thesis statement of a narrative essay that uses stories about teenage drunk driving incidents to argue in favor of students working to reduce the problem.

Step Five: Write an outline or diagram.

1. Write the thesis statement at the top of the outline.
2. Write numerals I, II, and III on the left side of the page.

3. Next to each numeral, write down the best ideas you came up with in step three. These should all directly relate to and support the thesis statement.
4. Next to each letter write down information that supports that particular idea.

Step Six: Write the three supporting paragraphs.

Use your outline to write the three supporting paragraphs. Write down the main idea of each paragraph in sentence form. Do the same thing for the supporting points of information. Each sentence should support the paragraph of the topic. Be sure you have relevant and interesting details, facts, and quotes. Use transitions when you move from idea to idea to keep the text fluid and smooth. Sometimes, although not always, paragraphs can include a concluding or summary sentence that restates the paragraph's argument.

Step Seven: Write the introduction and conclusion.

See Exercise 3B for information on writing introductions and conclusions.

Step Eight: Read and rewrite.

As you read, check your essay for the following:

✔ Does the essay maintain a consistent tone?
✔ Do all paragraphs reinforce your general thesis?
✔ Do all paragraphs flow from one to the other? Do you need to add transition words or phrases?
✔ Have you quoted from reliable, authoritative, and interesting sources?
✔ Is there a sense of progression throughout the essay?
✔ Does the essay get bogged down in too much detail or irrelevant material?
✔ Does your introduction grab the reader's attention?
✔ Does your conclusion reflect back on any previously discussed material, or give the essay a sense of closure?
✔ Are there any spelling or grammatical errors?

Section Three:
Supporting
Research
Material

Facts About Drunk Driving

Editor's Note: These facts can be used in reports or papers to add credibility when making important points or claims.

Drunk Driving in the United States

- States with the highest rates of fatal alcohol-related crashes are Alaska (52.8 percent), Texas (49.8 percent), North Dakota (47.8 percent), Massachusetts (47.4 percent), and Arizona (45.5 percent).
- States with the lowest rates of fatal alcohol-related crashes are Utah (20.6 percent), New York (27.4 percent), Arkansas (29.2 percent), Kansas (29.5 percent), and Wyoming (31.5 percent).

According to the U.S. Department of Transportation:

- There is an alcohol-related traffic fatality every thirty-one minutes and an alcohol-related traffic injury every two minutes.
- About 1.5 million drivers are arrested for driving each year under the influence of alcohol or narcotics.
- There is about one alcohol- or narcotics-related driving arrest for every 137 licensed drivers in the United States.

According to the organization Alcohol Alert:

- Motor vehicle crashes are the leading cause of death of Americans ages five to thirty-five, and more than 50 percent of these accidents are caused by alcohol-impaired drivers.
- One American life is lost every twenty minutes in alcohol-related auto crashes.
- It is estimated that three out of every ten Americans (30 percent) will be involved in an alcohol-related accident in his or her lifetime.

- Over 394,000 people have died in alcohol related accidents in the past twenty years.
- More than three hundred people are killed each week in alcohol-related accidents.
- More than forty-five people are killed each day in alcohol-related accidents.

According to the Centers for Disease Control and Prevention:

- In 2005, 16,885 people in the United States died in alcohol-related motor vehicle crashes, representing 39 percent of all traffic-related deaths.
- In 2005, nearly 1.4 million drivers were arrested for driving under the influence of alcohol or narcotics. That's less than 1 percent of the 159 million self-reported episodes of alcohol–impaired driving among U.S. adults each year.
- More than half of the 414 child passengers ages fourteen and younger who died in alcohol-related crashes during 2005 were riding with the drinking driver.

Teenage Drunk Driving

- According to the organization Alcohol Alert, alcohol-related crashes are the leading cause of death for young Americans between the ages of sixteen and twenty-four years old.
- According to the National Highway Traffic Safety Administration, in 2005, 16 percent of drivers ages sixteen to twenty who died in motor vehicle crashes had been drinking alcohol.
- At all levels of blood alcohol concentration, the risk of being involved in a crash is greater for young people than for older people.
- The United States has the world's highest drinking age.

- According to the National Highway Traffic Safety Administration, motor vehicle crashes are the number one cause of death among youth ages fifteen to twenty.
- According to the Core Institute at Southern Illinois University, 27 percent of college students drive under the influence of alcohol—this is about 2 million college students.
- Fifty-two percent of male college students and 35 percent of female college students binge drink occasionally or regularly, according to the University of Michigan Health System.
- An estimated 110,000 students between the ages of eighteen and twenty-four are arrested for an alcohol-related violation such as public drunkenness or driving under the influence each year.

According to the Insurance Institute on Highway Safety:
- In 2004, 26 percent of sixteen-to-twenty-year-old passenger vehicle drivers fatally injured in crashes had high blood alcohol concentrations (0.08 percent or higher).
- The percentage of fatally injured drivers with high blood alcohol concentrations was lower among female teenagers (14 percent) than among male teenagers (31 percent).

Blood Alcohol Content (BAC) Levels
- A BAC of .02–.05 causes relaxation, slight body warmth, and lower inhibition.
- A BAC of .05–.10 causes impairment of speech, vision, balance; sedation; slower reaction time; and reduced self-control.
- A BAC of .10–.20 causes slurred speech, blurred vision, poor coordination, loss of balance, slowed thinking, and nausea.

- A BAC of .20–.30 causes difficulty walking, mental confusion, double vision, and vomiting.
- A BAC of .30–.40 causes a person to pass out and experience tremors, memory loss, and a lowered body temperature.
- A BAC of .40–.50 causes difficulty breathing, coma, and possible death.
- A BAC of .50 and up causes death.

According to the National Highway Traffic Safety Administration:
- About half of all drivers arrested and half of those convicted of driving under the influence have BAC levels of 0.15 or above.
- The most frequently recorded BAC level of drivers involved in fatal crashes is 0.18.
- A person with a BAC level of 0.15 or higher is twenty times more likely than a sober driver to be in a fatal car accident.

According to the National Hardcore Drunk Driver Project:
- A driver with a 0.15 BAC is 385 times more likely to be involved in a fatal crash than a driver with a BAC of zero.

Groups at Risk
- Male drivers involved in fatal motor vehicle crashes are almost twice as likely as female drivers to be intoxicated with a BAC of 0.08 or greater.
- Male drivers between twenty-two and forty-five years old are responsible for almost 50 percent of all drunk driving crashes.
- According to the organization Alcohol Alert, males (31 percent) are more than twice as likely as females (13 percent) to report driving after drinking. They also consume more alcohol before driving.

Seat Belts and Alcohol

According to the Loyola University Health System:

- Safety belts were used by approximately 12.8 percent of fatally injured intoxicated drivers as compared to 33 percent of sober drivers killed in crashes.
- Drivers involved in fatal crashes who have been drinking use safety belts at a substantially lower rate than sober drivers.

Sobriety Checkpoints

- Less than 1 percent of drivers stopped at sobriety checkpoints in Pennsylvania during 2001 were charged with driving under the influence.
- Officials in Brevard County, Florida, credit sobriety checkpoints with reducing alcohol-related traffic fatalities by 38.2 percent.
- As of January 2006, sobriety checkpoints are allowed in thirty-nine states, the District of Columbia, and Puerto Rico.
- Iowa, Idaho, Michigan, Minnesota, Montana, Oregon, Rhode Island, Texas, Washington, Wisconsin, and Wyoming do not allow sobriety checkpoints.

According to Mothers Against Drunk Driving:

- Sobriety checkpoints can reduce alcohol-related crashes and fatalities by 20 percent.
- Seventy to eighty percent of Americans favor sobriety checkpoint use to combat drunk driving.
- Well-conducted sobriety checkpoints generally delay drivers for no more than thirty seconds and cause no traffic problems.

Finding and Using Sources of Information

No matter what type of essay you are writing, it is necessary to find information to support your point of view. You can use sources such as books, magazine articles, newspaper articles, and online articles.

Using Books and Articles

You can find books and articles in a library by using the library's computer or cataloging system. If you are not sure how to use these resources, ask a librarian to help you. You can also use a computer to find many magazine articles and other articles written specifically for the Internet.

You are likely to find a lot more information than you can possibly use in your essay, so your first task is to narrow the information down to what is likely to be most usable. Look at book and article titles. Look at book chapter titles and examine the book's index to see if it contains information on the specific topic you want to write about. (For example, if you want to write about sobriety checkpoints, and you find a book about alcohol, check the chapter titles and index to be sure it contains information about sobriety checkpoints before you bother to check out the book.)

For a five-paragraph essay, you do not need a great deal of supporting information, so quickly try to narrow down your materials to a few good books, magazines or Internet articles. You do not need dozens. You might even find that one or two good books or articles contain all the information you need.

You probably do not have time to read an entire book, so find the chapters or sections that relate to your topic, and skim these. When you find useful information, copy it onto a note card or notebook. You should look for supporting facts, statistics, quotations, and examples.

Using the Internet

When you select your supporting information, it is important that you evaluate its source. This is especially important with information you find on the Internet. Because nearly anyone can put information on the Internet, there is as much bad information as good information. Before using Internet information—or any information—try to determine if the source is reliable. Is the author or Internet site sponsored by a legitimate organization? Is the information from a government source? Does the author have any special knowledge or training relating to the topic you are looking up? Does the article give any indication of where its information comes from?

Using Your Supporting Information

When you use supporting information from a book, article, interview, or other source, there are three important things to remember:

1. *Make it clear whether you are using a direct quotation or a paraphrase.* If you copy information directly from your source, you are quoting it. You must put quotation marks around the information, and tell where the information comes from. If you put the information in your own words, you are paraphrasing it.

   Here is an example of a using a quotation:
   Author Radley Balko believes that the problem of drunk driving is exaggerated, and laws to prevent it punish the wrong people. "Our laws should be grounded in sound science and the presumption of innocence, not in hysteria. They should target repeat offenders and severely impaired drunks, not social drinkers who straddle the legal threshold."

Here is an example of a brief paraphrase of the same passage:

> Author Radley Balko believes that the problem of drunk driving is exaggerated, and laws to prevent it punish the wrong people. He argues that current drunk driving laws target social drinkers who pose no threat to society instead of going after hard-core drunk drivers and repeat offenders.

2. *Use the information fairly.* Be careful to use supporting information in the way the author intended it. For example, it is unfair to quote an author as saying, "Ignition interlock devices should be mandatory for all" when he or she intended to say, "Ignition interlock devices should be mandatory for all first-time offenders." This is called taking information out of context. This is using supporting evidence unfairly.

3. *Give credit where credit is due.* Giving credit is known as citing. You must use citations when you use someone else's information, but not every piece of supporting information needs a citation.

   - If the supporting information is general knowledge— that is, it can be found in many sources—you do not have to cite your source.
   - If you directly quote a source, you must cite it.
   - If you paraphrase information from a specific source, you must cite it.

If you do not use citations where you should, you are *plagiarizing*—or stealing—someone else's work.

Citing Your Sources

There are a number of ways to cite your sources. Your teacher will probably want you to do it in one of three ways:

- Informal: As in the example in number 1 above, tell where you got the information as you present it in the text of your essay.
- Informal list: At the end of your essay, place an unnumbered list of all the sources you used. This tells the reader where, in general, your information came from.
- Formal: Use numbered footnotes. Footnotes are generally placed at the end of an article or essay, although they may be placed elsewhere depending on your teacher's requirements.

Works Cited

Balko, Radley. "Drunk Driving Laws Are Out of Control." *Cato Institute* 27 July 2004.

Using MLA Style to Create a Works Cited List

You will probably need to create a list of works cited for your paper. These include materials that you quoted from, relied heavily on, or consulted to write your paper. There are several different ways to structure these references. The following examples are based on Modern Language Association (MLA) style, one of the major citation styles used by writers.

Book Entries

For most book entries you will need the author's name, the book's title, where it was published, what company published it, and the year it was published. This information is usually found on the inside of the book. Variations on book entries include the following:

A book by a single author:
> Guest, Emma. *Children of AIDS: Africa's Orphan Crisis.* London: Sterling, 2003.

Two or more books by the same author:
> Friedman, Thomas L. *The World Is Flat: A Brief History of the Twentieth Century.* New York: Farrar, Straus and Giroux, 2005.

> ---. *From Beirut to Jerusalem.* New York: Doubleday, 1989.

A book by two or more authors:
> Pojman, Louis P., and Jeffrey Reiman. *The Death Penalty: For and Against.* Lanham, MD: Rowman & Littlefield, 1998.

A book with an editor:
> Friedman, Lauri S., ed. *At Issue: What Motivates Suicide Bombers?* San Diego, CA: Greenhaven, 2004.

Periodical and Newspaper Entries

Entries for sources found in periodicals and newspapers are cited a bit differently than books. For one, these sources usually have a title and a publication name. They also may have specific dates and page numbers. Unlike book entries, you do not need to list where newspapers or periodicals are published or what company publishes them.

An Article from a Periodical:
> Snow, Keith Harmon. "State Terror in Ethiopia." *Z Magazine* June 2004: 33–35.

An Unsigned Article from a Periodical:
> "Broadcast Decency Rules." *Issues & Controversies on File* 30 Apr. 2004.

An Article from a Newspaper:
> Constantino, Rebecca. "Fostering Love, Respecting Race." *Los Angeles Times* 14 Dec. 2002: B17.

Internet Sources

To document a source you found online, try to provide as much information on it as possible, including the author's name, the title of the document, date of publication or of last revision, the URL, and your date of access.

A Web Source:
> Shyovitz, David. "The History and Development of Yiddish." Jewish Virtual Library. 30 May 2005 http://www.jewishvirtuallibrary.org/jsource/History/yiddish.html. Accessed September 11, 2007.

Your teacher will tell you exactly how information should be cited in your essay. Generally, the very least information needed is the original author's name and the name of the article or other publication.

Be sure you know exactly what information your teacher requires before you start looking for your supporting information so that you know what information to include with your notes.

Sample Essay Topics

Drunk Driving Is a Serious Problem

The Problem of Drunk Driving Is Overstated

Drunk Driving Is Increasing

Drunk Driving Is Declining

There Should Be Harsher Punishments for Drunk Driving

Punishments Are Harsh Enough for Drunk Driving

Opening SADD Chapters in Schools Can Prevent Drunk Driving

Alcohol and Drug Education Classes Can Prevent Drunk Driving

Society Is Too Complacent About Drunk Driving

Society Overreacts to Drunk Driving

Alcohol Monitoring Devices Can Reduce Drunk Driving

Alcohol Monitoring Devices Are Not Foolproof

Alcohol Monitoring Devices Are a Violation of Civil Liberties

Sobriety Checkpoints Reduce Drunk Driving

Sobriety Checkpoints Do Not Reduce Drunk Driving

Enforcing Underage Drinking Laws Can Reduce Drunk Driving

A Higher Drinking Age Can Reduce Drunk Driving

A Lower Drinking Age Can Promote Responsible Drinking and Driving

Blood Alcohol Content Limits Should Be Lowered

Blood Alcohol Content Limits Should Be Raised

Ignition Interlock Devices Can Reduce Drunk Driving

Ignition Interlock Devices Cannot Effectively Reduce Drunk Driving

Writing Prompts for Personal Narratives

Use another person's story or your own story to illustrate any of the topics listed here, or come up with a unique topic on your own. Describe what happened during an incident when you, a person you know, or someone you read about was in a situation that involved drunk driving. Use research, interviews, or personal experience to tell the story so that it supports the point you want to make about drunk driving.

Organizations to Contact

Advocates for Highway and Auto Safety

750 First Street NE, Suite 901, Washington, DC 20002 • (202) 408-1711 • fax: (202) 408-1699 • e-mail: advocates@saferoads.org • Web site: www.saferoads.org

Advocates for Highway and Auto Safety is an alliance of consumer, health, and safety groups, and insurance companies that encourages adoption of laws, policies, and programs that save lives and reduce injuries. The group's Web site has information and news on a variety of highway safety issues, including drunk driving and teen driving.

Alcoholics Anonymous (AA)

General Service Office PO Box 459, Grand Central Station, New York, NY 10163 • (212) 870-3400 • fax: (212) 870-3003 • Web site: www.aa.org

Alcoholics Anonymous (AA) is an international fellowship of people who are recovering from alcoholism. Because AA's primary goal is to help alcoholics remain sober, it does not sponsor research or engage in education about alcoholism. AA does, however, publish a catalog of literature concerning the organization as well as several pamphlets, including *Is AA for You? Young People and AA, and A Brief Guide to Alcoholics Anonymous.*

American Beverage Institute (ABI)

1775 Pennsylvania Avenue NW, Suite 1200, Washington, DC 20006 • (202) 463-7110 • Web site: www.abionline.org

The American Beverage Institute is a restaurant industry trade organization that works to protect the right to consume alcoholic beverages in the restaurant setting. It unites the wine, beer, and spirits producers with distributors and on-premise retailers in this effort. It conducts research and education in an attempt to demonstrate that the vast majority of adults who drink alcohol outside of the home are responsible, law-abiding citizens. Its Web site includes fact sheets and news articles on various issues, such as drunk driving laws, alcohol taxes, and research reports including *The Anti-Drunk Driving Campaign: A Covert War Against Drinking and The .08 Debate: What's the Harm?*

American Society of Addiction Medicine (ASAM)

4601 North Park Avenue, Upper Arcade #101, Chevy Chase, MD 20815 • (301) 656-3920 • fax: (301) 656-3815 • e-mail: email@asam.org • Web site: www.asam.org

The American Society of Addiction Medicine is the nation's addiction medicine specialty society dedicated to educating physicians and improving the treatment of individuals suffering from alcoholism and other addictions. In addition, the organization promotes research and prevention of addiction and works for the establishment of addiction medicine as a specialty recognized by the American Board of Medical Specialties. The organization publishes medical texts and a bimonthly newsletter.

The Beer Institute

122 C Street NW, Suite 750, Washington, DC 20001 • (202) 737-2337 • e-mail: info@beerinstitute.org • Web site: www.beerinstitute.org

The Beer Institute is a trade organization that represents the beer industry before Congress, state legislatures, and public forums across the country. It sponsors educational programs to prevent underage drinking and drunk driving and distributes fact sheets and news briefs on issues such as alcohol taxes and advertising. Its *Beer Institute Bulletin* newsletter is published four times a year.

Campaign Against Drunk Driving (CADD)

PO Box 62, Brighouse, West Yorkshire HD6 3YY •
0845-123-5541 • e-mail: add@scard.org.uk • Web site:
www.cadd.org.uk

Campaign Against Drunk Driving is a British organization
dedicating to providing support to victims of drunk driving
and to promoting stronger drunk driving laws, including
a lower BAC level. Its Web site provides sources for drunk
driving statistics in Great Britain.

Center for Science in the Public Interest (CSPI)

1875 Connecticut Avenue NW, Suite 300, Washington,
DC 20009 • (202) 332-9110 • fax: (202) 265-4954 •
e-mail: cspi@cspinet.org • Web site: www.cspinet.org

The Center for Science in the Public Interest is an advocacy
organization that promotes nutrition and health, food safety, alcohol policy, and sound science. It favors the imple-
mentation of public policies aimed at reducing alcohol-
related problems, such as restricting alcohol advertising,
increasing alcohol taxes, and reducing drunk driving.

The Century Council

1310 G Street NW, Suite 600, Washington, DC 20005 •
(202) 637-0077 • fax: (202) 637-0079 • e-mail: kimballl@
centurycouncil.org • Web site: www.centurycouncil.org

A nonprofit organization funded by America's liquor
industry, the Century Council's mission is to fight drunk
driving and underage drinking. It promotes responsible
decision-making about drinking and discourages all forms
of irresponsible alcohol consumption through education, communications, research, law enforcement, and
other programs. Its Web site offers fact sheets and other
resources on drunk driving, underage drinking, and other
alcohol-related problems.

Distilled Spirits Council of the United States (DISCUS)

1250 I Street NW, Suite 900, Washington, DC 20005 • (202) 628-3544 • Web site: www.discus.org

The Distilled Spirits Council of the United States (DISCUS) is the national trade association representing producers and marketers of distilled spirits in the United States. It seeks to ensure the responsible advertising and marketing of distilled spirits to adult consumers and to prevent such advertising and marketing from targeting individuals below the legal purchase age. DISCUS publishes fact sheets, news releases, and documents, including its semi-annual report, *Code of Responsible Practices for Beverage Alcohol Advertising and Marketing.*

Insurance Institute for Highway Safety (IIHS)

1005 North Glebe Road, Suite 800, Arlington, VA 22201 • (703) 247-1500 • fax: (703) 247-1588 • Web site: www.iihs.org

The Insurance Institute for Highway Safety (IIHS) is a scientific and educational organization dedicated to reducing the losses—deaths, injuries, and property damage—from crashes on the nation's highways. IIHS's Web site contains research and statistics on drunk driving and information on laws about drunk driving in all fifty states.

International Center for Alcohol Policies (ICAP)

1519 New Hampshire Avenue, NW, Washington, DC 20036 • (202) 986-1159 • fax: (202) 986-2080 • Web site: www.icap.org

The International Center for Alcohol Policies (ICAP) is a nonprofit organization dedicated to helping reduce the abuse of alcohol worldwide and to promote understanding of the role of alcohol in society through dialogue and partnerships involving the beverage industry, the public health community, and others interested in alcohol policy.

ICAP is supported by eleven major international beverage alcohol companies.

Mothers Against Drunk Driving (MADD)

511 East John Carpenter Freeway, No. 700, Irving, TX 75062 • 800-GET-MADD (438-6233) • fax: (972) 869-2206/07 • e-mail: Information: info@madd.org • Victim's Assistance: victims@madd.org • Web site: www.madd.org

Mothers Against Drunk Driving (MADD) seeks to act as the voice of victims of drunk driving accidents by speaking on their behalf to communities, businesses, and educational groups and by providing materials for use in medical facilities and health and driver education programs. MADD publishes the biannual magazine *MADDvocate* for victims and their advocates and the newsletter *MADD in Action* as well as a variety of fact sheets, brochures, and other materials on drunk driving.

National Center on Addiction and Substance Abuse (CASA)

633 Third Avenue, Nineteenth Floor, New York, NY 10017 • (212) 841-5200 • Web site: www.casacolumbia.org

The National Center on Addiction and Substance Abuse (CASA) is a nonprofit organization affiliated with Columbia University. It works to educate the public about the problems of substance abuse and addiction and to evaluate prevention, treatment, and law enforcement programs to address the problem. Its Web site contains reports and op-ed articles on alcohol policy and the alcohol industry, including the reports *Teen Tipplers: America's Underage Drinking Epidemic* and *The Economic Value of Underage and Adult Excessive Drinking to the Alcohol Industry*.

National Commission Against Drunk Driving (NCADD)

8403 Colesville Road, Suite 370, Silver Spring, MD 20910 • (240) 247-6004 • fax: (240) 247-7012 • e-mail: info@ncadd.com • Web site: www.ncadd.com

The National Commission Against Drunk Driving is a coalition of public and private organizations and others who work together to reduce impaired driving and its tragic consequences. Its Web site has a searchable database offering abstracts of research studies, which is an excellent research resource.

National Highway Traffic Safety Administration (NHTSA)

400 Seventh Street SW, Washington, DC 20590 • (888) 327-4236 • Web site: www.nhtsa.dot.gov

The National Highway Traffic Safety Administration (NHTSA) is a department within the U.S. Department of Transportation. It is responsible for reducing deaths, injuries, and economic losses resulting from motor vehicle crashes. It sets and enforces safety performance standards for motor vehicles and motor vehicle equipment and awards grants to state and local governments to enable them to conduct local highway safety programs. The NHTSA publishes information on drunk driving, including a list of tips titled "Get the Keys: How You Can Intervene" and the publication *Strategies for Success: Combating Juvenile DUI*.

National Institute on Alcoholism and Alcohol Abuse (NIAAA)

5635 Fishers Lane, MSC 9304, Bethesda, MD 20892 • Web site: www.niaaa.nih.gov

The National Institute on Alcoholism and Alcohol Abuse (NIAAA) is one of the eighteen institutes that comprise the National Institutes of Health. NIAAA provides leadership in the national effort to reduce alcohol-related problems such as drunk driving.

Responsibility in DUI Laws, Inc. (RIDL)
PO Box 87053, Canton, MI 48188 • e-mail: info@ridl.us • Web site: www.ridl.us

Responsibility in DUI Laws, Inc. (RIDL) believes current driving under the influence laws are too harsh and are aimed more at criminalizing and punishing responsible drinkers than curbing drunk driving. RIDL's mission is to educate the public and lawmakers about the misdirection of the current laws, take the steps necessary to get the current laws repealed, and to provide alternative suggestions for dealing with the problem of drunk driving.

Students Against Destructive Decisions (SADD)
SADD National
255 Main Street, Marlborough, MA 01752 • (877) SADDINC • fax: (508) 481-5759 • e-mail: info@sadd.org • Web site: www.sadd.org

Originally called Students Against Drunk Driving, this organization expanded its mission to provide students with the best prevention and intervention tools possible to deal with the issues of underage drinking, other drug use, impaired driving, and other destructive decisions. Now Students Against Destructive Decisions (SADD), its Web site has statistics on teens and drunk driving along with information on how to form local SADD chapters.

University of North Carolina Highway Safety Research Center
CB# 3430 Chapel Hill, NC 27599 • (919) 962-2202 or (800) 672-4527 • fax: (919) 962-8710 • Web site: www.hsrc.unc.edu

The University of North Carolina Highway Safety Research Center has conducted research aimed at reducing deaths, injuries, and related societal costs of roadway crashes.

Alcohol impairment and teen driving are among the areas addressed on its Web site.

U.S. Department of Transportation (DOT)
400 Seventh Street SW, Washington, DC 20590 •
(202) 366-4000 • Web site: www.dot.gov

The U.S. Department of Transportation (DOT) works to promote fast, safe, efficient, convenient, and accessible transportation in the U.S. It's Web site offers articles and reports by the DOT and other government agencies about drunk driving.

Bibliography

Books

Dennis A. Bjorklund, *Drunk Driving Laws: Rules of the Road When Crossing State Lines*. Praetorian, 2005.

Spencer G. Markle, *Drunk Driving: What to Do When Your Family Is Victimized*. Spencer G. Markle, 2006.

Emil Steiner, *Drunk Driving*. Frederick, MD: PublishAmerica, 2005.

Doug Thorburn, *Get Out of the Way! How to Identify and Avoid a Driver Under the Influence*. Northridge, CA: Galt, 2002.

Christine van Tuyl, *Issues That Concern You: Drunk Driving*. Farmington Hills, MI: Greenhaven Press, 2006.

Mike Wilson, *Introducing with Opposing Viewpoints: Drunk Driving*. Farmington Hills, MI: Greenhaven Press, 2006.

Periodicals

Catherine Arnst, "The Deadliest Drunk-Driving States: A Doctor-led Group Ranks the States with the Highest and Lowest Rates of Drunk-driving Fatalities," *Business Week Online,* December 4, 2006.

Radley Balko, "Drunk Driving Laws Are Out of Control," Cato Institute, July 27, 2004.

Patrick T. Barone, "Alcohol Monitoring Ankle Bracelets: Junk Science or Important Scientific Breakthrough?" *Champion,* May 2005.

Kim Bell, "Ankle Bracelet Can Catch DWI Offenders Who Cheat," *St. Louis Post-Dispatch,* January 23, 2006.

Bloomberg School of Public Health, "Alcohol Drinkers Three Times as Likely to Die from Injury," Ascribe Health News Service, February 10, 2005.

"Breathing Problems: Should Teens Be Required to Take Breathalyzer Tests?" *Current Events,* October 7, 2005.

Michael Christie, "A Seatbelt That Says You're Too Drunk to Drive; Volvo Device Hits Ignition," *Daily Record,* September 7, 2005.

John Cichowski, "Drinking and Driving: Should Laws Get Tougher? *Record,* November 23, 2005.

David J. DeYoung, Helen N. Tashima, and Scott V. Masten, *An Evaluation of the Effectiveness of Ignition Interlock in California,* Report to the Legislature of the State of California, September 2004.

John Doyle, "Sobriety Checkpoints Are Intrusive and Wasteful," *Record* (New Jersey), December 19, 2005.

"Drunk Driving's Toll: Drinking and Driving Is Deadly. It's Time to Crack Down," *Charlotte Observer,* March 15, 2006.

David J. Hanson, "The Drinking Age Should Be Lowered: Interview with Dr. Ruth Engs," Alcohol Problems and Solutions. www2.potsdam.edu/hansondj/YouthIssues/1053520190.html.

David Hench, "Homeward Bound: Kate Bishop, Confined to Her Home for Paralyzing a Man While Driving Drunk, Tries to Educate Others," *Portland Press Herald,* November 1, 2004.

John Klopfer, "Lower the Drinking Age," *University Wire,* December 6, 2005.

Bruce Landis, "Bill Would Widen Interlock Use," *Providence Journal,* January 23, 2006.

Mitchell Ignatoff, "Tale of Two Standards in DWI Cases," *New Jersey Law Journal,* January 1, 2007.

Insurance Institute for Highway Safety, "Q & A: Teenagers—Underage Drinking," Insurance Institute for Highway Safety, 2006.

Nancy McVicar, "Calling While Driving as Dangerous as Driving Drunk," *South Florida Sun-Sentinel,* June 29, 2006.

Jeanne Mejeur, "Way Too Drunk to Drive," *State Legislatures,* December 1, 2005.

Haya el Nasser, "States Turn on to Idea of Ignition Locks," *USA Today,* June 23, 2005.

National Commission Against Drunk Driving, "What Research Says About Chronic Drinking Drivers and Ways to Apply This Research," National Commission Against Drunk Driving, 2006.

National Conference of State Legislatures, "If You're Going to Drive Drunk, Leave the Kids at Home," National Conference of State Legislatures, July 28, 2005.

National Highway Traffic Safety Administration, "Small Scale Sobriety Checkpoints," National Highway Traffic Safety Administration, 2006.

Rick Popely, "Drunken Driving Gains Level Off Despite Tougher Laws," *Chicago Tribune,* November 26, 2004.

Gina Stoduto, "The Criminalization of Impaired Driving in Canada: Assessing the Deterrent Impact of Canada's First Per Se Law," *Journal of Studies on Alcohol,* July 1, 2004.

Lawrence Taylor, "Technology Alone Won't Tackle Drunk Driving; Ignition Interlock Devices Promoted by MADD Will Do Little to Stop People from Driving while Intoxicated." *Business Week Online,* December 4, 2006.

Libby Tucker, "Fatal Choice: Keith Wagner Was 15 Years Old When He Died in a Car Incident," *Scholastic Choices,* January 2007.

Robert Voas, "There's No Benefit to Lowering the Drinking Age," *Christian Science Monitor,* January 12, 2006.

Allison Hope Weiner and Joshua Rich, "The Year of Living Dangerously," *Entertainment Weekly*, December 8, 2006.

Debbie Weir, "From This Day Forward," *MADDvocate*, Spring 2006.

Louis Wittig, "Under the Influence of Celebrity; Hollywood's Blind Spot for Drunk Driving," *Weekly Standard*, January 29, 2007.

Web Sites

Alcohol Alert (www.alcoholalert.com). Contains useful statistics about drunk driving and several articles on breathalyzer technology.

DUI.com (www.dui.com). A comprehensive Web site containing state-by-state driving under the influence laws, first-offender penalties, and drunk-driving prevention technologies.

National Hardcore Drunk Driver Project (http://dwi-data.org). A project of the Century Council whose goal is to protect the public by reducing the recidivism of hardcore drunk drivers.

Orillia Against Drunk Driving (OADD) (www.oadd.ca/index.html). A community-based nonprofit organization that works to reduce and eliminate drinking and driving. OADD was formed in November 1994 in memoriam of 15-year-old Tim Abernethy who was killed by a drunk driver.

People Affected by Drunk Driving (PADD) (www.padd1.org). A Web site for victims of drunk drivers.

Index

Crash. *See* Accident
Crash Outcome Data
  Evaluation System
  Intermountain Injury
  Control Research
  Center, 17
Curfew, 32–34

Death, *See* Fatalities
Desert Morning News, 13
Diagram. *See* outline
Dialogue, 70, 74
Distilled Spirits Council
  of the United States
  (DICUS), 97
Drinking
  binge, 13, 16, 28–29
  consequences, 60–62,
    70–72, 74, 81, 83, 98
  guilt, 21–27, 48–50
  laws, 29, 31–32, 92,
    95–96, 103
  risks, 9, 18, 20, 26,
    35–36, 38, 47, 84
  underage, 13–16, 31,
    100
Driver's license, 30–32,
  60
Drugs, 17, 30, 62
Drunk driver character-
  istics, 34
Drunk driving
  teenagers, 13, 15–18

Drunk driving
  facts, 80–84
  fatalities, 7, 21–27,
    38–41
  observations, 77–78
  penalties, 7, 11, 14,
    48–49, 50, 53, 60
  prevention, 7–8, 11,
    28 35
DUI (driving under the
  influence), DWI (driving
  while intoxicated), 7,
  17, 23–24, 26, 55

Educators, 5, 15
Elementary schools, 5,
  15, 17
Environmental factors,
  8–9
Essay
  action, 65–66
  evaluation, 48, 64–65
  outline, 52–53, 57
  pivotal events, 65–67
  point/moral, 66
  rules, 5–6, 44–45
  topics, 92
Essay parts
  character, 46–47, 61,
    64–65, 70–71
  conclusion, 44, 59,
    67–68, 73, 78
  setting, 46–47, 61,
    64–65, 70–71

Picture Credits

About the Editor

Lauri S. Friedman earned her bachelor's degree in religion and political science from Vassar College in Poughkeepsie, NY. Her studies there focused on political Islam. Friedman has worked as a non-fiction writer, a newspaper journalist, and an editor for more than 7 years. She has accumulated extensive experience in both academic and professional settings.

Friedman has edited and authored numerous publications for Greenhaven Press on controversial social issues such as gay marriage, Islam, energy, discrimination, suicide bombers, and the war on terror. Much of the Writing the Critical Essay series has been under her direction or authorship. She was instrumental in the creation of the series, and played a critical role in its conception and development.